A

CATALOGUE

OF

THE PLANTS

OF

THE PUNJAB AND SINDH

A CATALOGUE OF THE PLANTS OF THE PUNJAB AND SINDH.

JAMES EDWARD TIERNEY AITCHISON, M. D.

GYAN

Published by

Gyan Publishing House
5, Ansari Road
Daryaganj, New Delhi-110002
Phone: 011-47034999, 9811692060
E-mail: books@gyanbooks.com

Distribution Network
gyanbooks.com
India, USA, Canada, UK, Australia, France

ISBN: 978-81-212-8358-8 (PB)
First Published, 1869

2nd Impression 2023

Printed at: Gyan Press, Delhi.

A CATALOGUE OF THE PLANTS OF THE PUNJAB AND SINDH
Author: JAMES EDWARD TIERNEY AITCHISON

A CATALOGUE OF THE PLANTS OF THE PUNJAB AND SINDH.

TO WHICH ARE ADDED

SOME OTHERS

THAT, FROM THEIR PRESENT GEOGRAPHICAL PROXIMITY, MAY BE FOUND HEREAFTER TO OCCUR IN THE PUNJAB.

BY

JAMES EDWARD TIERNEY AITCHISON, M.D.,

MEMBER OF THE ROYAL COLLEGE OF PHYSICIANS, EDIN.; FELLOW OF THE ROYAL COLLEGE OF SURGEONS, EDIN.;
FELLOW OF THE LINNEAN SOCIETY OF LONDON;
CORRESPONDING FELLOW OF THE OBSTETRICAL SOCIETY OF EDINBURGH;
ASSISTANT-SURGEON IN HER MAJESTY'S BENGAL ARMY; AND
LATELY CIVIL SURGEON OF JHELUM, HUSHIARPUR, AND UMRITSUR IN THE PUNJAB.

LONDON:

PUBLISHED BY TAYLOR AND FRANCIS FOR THE AUTHOR,

AND SOLD AT

THE AMERICAN MISSION PRESS, LOODIANA, PUNJAB, INDIA.

1869.

PREFACE.

In the preparation of the accompanying 'Catalogue of the Plants of the Punjab,' I have (in addition to my own collections) made use of the following published materials :—

1. Hooker and Thomson's 'Flora Indica,' vol. i., with its continuation in the "Præcursores" published in the 'Proceedings of Linnean Society' (vols. ii.–v.).

2. Royle's 'Illustrations of the Botany of the Himalaya.'

3. Griffith's 'Itinerary' and 'Posthumous Papers,' published by the Government of India.

4. Various Monographs in the 'Transactions' and 'Proceedings' of the Linnean Society, in Hooker's 'Journal of Botany,' and the 'Journal of the Asiatic Society of Calcutta,' including Dr. T. Anderson's "East-Indian Acanthaceæ," Mr. Edgeworth's "Botanical and Agricultural Account of the Seikh Protected States," and his "Flora Mallica" (Multan Flora), General Munro's "Bambusæ," Professor Oliver's "Aurantiaceæ," Dr. J. L. Stewart's "Flora of Peshaur," Dr. Stocks's papers on the "Botany of Sindh and Beluchistan," and my own lists of Jhelum and Hushiarpur Plants.

I have also been permitted to consult that most valuable MS. Catalogue, prepared by Dr. Joseph Hooker at the time of the distribution of the East-Indian collection, known as Herb. Ind. Or. H. f. & T., including not only all the plants collected by himself and Dr. Thomson, but also all the Indian plants of the Hookerian Herbarium, among which those of Lady Dalhousie, Jacquemont, Griffith, Stocks, Vicary, Fleming, Strachey, Winterbottom, and Stewart are the most important for the present purpose.

A MS. list of Dr. Thomson's earlier collections in Rohilkhand

and the Punjab, and a Catalogue of Dr. Stocks's plants, given by him to Mr. Edgeworth, have also afforded useful information.

I have carefully compared my collections with the Kew Herbarium (which, in addition to the Indian plants already mentioned, now contains a complete set of Royle's plants, and of those of Dr. Falconer), and have had the most free use of Mr. Edgeworth's private collections, the whole of which (Ranunculaceæ, Grasses, and Ferns excepted) I have thoroughly examined.

In every case of doubt these Herbaria were consulted.

Here I must thank Dr. Thomson, who aided me in going over no less than 300 species in the Kew Herbarium, when I myself was not able to elucidate what was required. The labour and trouble he went through cannot be sufficiently estimated, except by one who has worked with and at such a large collection of plants as that at Kew.

Indeed without the immense and valuable assistance given me, by my being allowed to use the Catalogues and Herbaria of Dr. Joseph Hooker, Mr. Edgeworth, and Dr. T. Thomson, this list of all the known Punjab plants would certainly not have been nearly so complete as it now is.

To Professor Oliver I am greatly indebted for the frequent calls I made upon his time, and the trouble he took in helping me in the determination of many specimens.

Had I had the time to critically re-examine my list, no doubt it would have enhanced its value; but this could not be done, and I therefore lay it in its present condition before the public, hoping it may prove useful to some.

This Catalogue was nearly finished when I had the pleasure of seeing Dr. J. L. Stewart's 'Punjab Plants.' To it I would refer the reader for further localities of the more common and useful plants of the Punjab.

The plants of Sindh have been added to this list, principally on the authority of Stocks, Vicary, Frere, and Griffiths, very few having been collected by the author.

The further distribution of many species into the Superior-Gangetic Plain, Kumaon, Simla, Jamu, Afghanistan, and Beluchistan has been noted; and one or two species which, from their present geographical proximity, may be expected to occur within the limits of the Punjab proper have also been included.

By the Punjab, I understand that country that "extends from the northern border of Sindh and Marwar, or rather Jesalmir, to the base of the Himalaya, and from the mountains of Afghanistan, which skirt the right bank of the Indus, to the borders of the Gangetic plain. Strickly speaking, the river Sutlej, or Gharra, is the south-eastern boundary of the Punjab; but politically the Cis-Sutlej states have been attached to it; and for our purposes it is convenient to draw the boundary along the line which separates the waters tributary to the Ganges from those which flow toward the Indus.

"This line lies to the eastward of the river Gagar, whose channel may be traced by Bhatnir to the Sutlej, a little above Bahawalpur, though its waters are generally absorbed by the desert long before they reach that river. It therefore includes Bahawalpur and Bhatiana, as well as the Cis-Sutlej states."—*H. f. & T.* vol. i. p. 156, para. 16, 'Flora Indica.'

"Sindh.—The province of Sindh extends from the sea on the south to the borders of the Punjab on the north. Westwards it is bounded by the mountains of Beluchistan, and on the east it is continuous with the desert of Marwar.

"Sindh is an alluvial plain watered by the various branches of the Indus."—*H. f. & T.* vol. i. p. 151, para. 14, 'Flora Indica.'

J. E. TIERNEY AITCHISON.

ABBREVIATIONS.

Edgew....................	for	Edgeworth.
T. T....................	,,	Thomas Thomson.
H. f. & T....................	,,	Hooker filius and Thomson.
St. & Wint.	,,	Strachey and Winterbottom.
Jacq....................	,,	Jacquemont.
J. L. S....................	,,	John Lindsay Stewart.
Dalz....................	,,	Dalzell.
Wall.	,,	Wallich.
Blink.	,,	Blinkbonny.
A.	,,	Aitchison.
Griff.	,,	Griffith.

ERRATA.

Page 23, line 23, *for* Gummy bags *read* Gunny-bags.
,, 32, ,, 3, *for* Caltha *read* Catha.
,, 36, ,, 3, *for* Am *read* Alm.
,, 49, ,, 18, *for* Horse-grain *read* Horse-Gram.
,, 55, ,, 23, *for* A. serissa *read* Acacia serissa.
,, 103, ,, 8, *for* Ma-Kon *read* Mahou.
,, 140, ,, 24, *for* Mujnor *read* Mujnoo.
,, 140, ,, 24, *for* Banih *read* Baint.
,, 141, ,, 16, *for* Kungla *read* Mungla.
,, 145, ,, 32, *for* Onvirandra *read* Ouvirandra.
,, 148, ,, 31, *for* Discorea *read* Dioscorea.
,, 149, ,, 30, *for* Sempervirens *read* Sempervivum.
,, 162, *for* 1333 *read* 1343.
,, 167, *for* 1880 *read* 1380.
,, 171, line 24, *for* Hordeaceæ *read* Hordeæ.
,, 171, ,, 35, *for* "Durun" read *durum*.
,, 172, ,, 1, *for* Rottbœlliaceæ *read* Rottbœlliæ.
,, 172, *for* 1454 *read* 1424.

Introduce under line 21, page 175, Andropogon Sorghum, *Brot.*

CATALOGUE.

THALAMIFLORÆ.

RANUNCULACEÆ.

1. **Clematis Gouriana**, *Roxb.*
   A. Jhelum; Mount Tilla; Hushiarpur: called "Buker-bael."
   H. f. & T. At the base of the Himalaya, as far west as the river Jelam, and to the Mountains of Rajaori.

2. **C. orientalis**, *L.*
   J. L. S. Peshaur.
   H. f. & T. Marri, *Fleming*; Kashmir, *Jacqt.*

3. **Adonis æstivalis**, *L.*
   J. L. S. Peshaur (most probably this species and not *autumnalis*, L.).
   Griffith. Afghanistan.
   Stocks. Beluchistan.

4. **Ranunculus falcatus**, *L.*
   Ceratocephalus falcatus, *Pers.*
   J. L. S. Peshaur, 1200 ft. only once; abundant at 7000 ft., mountains north-west from Dehra-Ishmael-Khan.
   H. f. & T. Beluch.; Afghan.

5. **R. aquatilis**, *L.*
   Royle. In superior Gangetic plain at Seharanpur.
   A. Jhelum; Hushiarpur.
   J. L. S. Peshaur.
   H. f. & T. Beluch.; Afghan.; Punjab Himalaya.

6. **R. sceleratus**, *L.*
   H. f. & T. Everywhere amongst sand, near water, in the plains of Northern India.
   T. T. Lahore; *Edgeworth*, Multan.
   A. Jhelum; Hushiarpur.
   J. L. S. Peshaur.

7. **R. lætus**, *Wall.*
   R. distans, *Royle.*
   R. brevirostris, *Edgew.*

J. L. S. Peshaur.
H. f. & T. Common in the temperate Himalaya, from 3000 to 10,000 ft.

8. R. PENSYLVANICUS, *L.*
R. chinensis, *Bunge, H. f. & T.*
R. riparius, *Edgew. Linn. Trans.*
Edgew. Sutlej; Loodiana.

9. R. ARVENSIS, *L.*
J. L. S. Peshaur.
H. f. & T. Beluch.; Afghan.; Western temperate Himalaya, from Kashmir to Kumaon.

10. R. MURICATUS, *L.*
A. Jhelum, Hushiarpur.
J. L. S. Peshaur.
H. f. & T. In the plains of Northern India, up to an altitude of from 5000 to 6000 ft.; Beluch.; Afghan.; Punjab; Peshaur.

11. DELPHINIUM PENICILLATUM, *Bois.*
J. L. S. Low hills near Peshaur.
Vicary. Raul-pindee.
H. f. & T. In the arid mountains of North-west India; Beluch.

12. D. SANICULÆFOLIUM, *Bois.*
A. Jhelum; Mount Tilla.
H. f. & T. Punjab; hills near the Indus river, *Fleming.*

MAGNOLIACEÆ.

13. MICHELIA CHAMPACA, *L.*
A. Hushiarpur, cultivated: called "Champa."
H. f. & T. Indigenous in temperate Himalaya, Kumaon, and Nepal, *Wall.*

ANONACEÆ.

14. GUATTERIA LONGIFOLIA, *Wall.*
Uvaria longifolia, *Lamb., Roxb. Fl. Indica,* ii. p. 664.
Unona longifolia, *Dun.*
A. Hushiarpur, cultiv.
H. f. & T. Cult. in Bengal and scarcely beyond the tropics.

15. ANONA SQUAMOSA, *L.*
A. Hushiarpur, cult., "Shureefa" and "Seeta-phul," bears fruit well, but requires protection from the frost. This seems to be its northern limit.
H. f. & T. Cultivated everywhere in India, and often naturalized.

MENISPERMACEÆ.

16. Anamirta cocculus, *W. & A.*
Edgew. Multan, cultiv.

17. Cocculus Leæba, *DC.*, *Forsk.*
A. Jhelum.
Edgew. Multan; Ferozepur; Loodiana.
J. L. S. Peshaur.
H. f. & T. Arid jungles of Sindh, *Vicary*; Afghan., *Griffith.*

18. C. villosus, *DC.*
Edgew. Multan.
H. f. & T. Over all Hindostan and the Punjab even to the base of the Himalaya.
Stocks. Indus basin.

19. Cissampelos pareira, *L.*
C. convolvulacea, *Willd.*
Edgew. Loodiana; Sadhaura.
A. Jhelum; Hushiarpur.
H. f. & T. Throughout the plains of India and lower Himalaya most common, even to the river Jelam, not in the arid parts of Punjab, Sindh, or Afghan.
A. Hushiarpur: called "Zucum-yeat" and "Betindoo."

NYMPHÆACEÆ.

20. Nymphæa Lotus, *L.*, γ.
N. pubescens, *Willd.*
Edgew. Multan.
A. Jhelum (not *alba*, L.).
T. T. Lahore.
Stocks. Indus basin.

21. N. stellata, *Willd.*
Edgew. Sadhaura.
A. Jhelum; Hushiarpur.
H. f. & T. Most common throughout the whole of the plains.

22. Nelumbium speciosum, *Willd.*
Edgew. Multan; Amballa.
A. Jhelum; Hushiarpur.
J. L. S. Peshaur.
H. f. & T. Throughout India, always introduced.
Stocks. Indus basin.
A. Generally, if not always, cultivated throughout the Punjab. The nuts, leaves, stems of the leaves, and rhizomes are all bazar commodities.

PAPAVERACEÆ.

23. **Papaver dubium**, *L.*, var. *β.* **lævigatum.**
J. L. S. Peshaur.
H. f. & T. Beluch., *Stocks*; Afghan., *Griffith*; from Kumaon to Kashmir.

24. **P. somniferum**, *L.*
P. album, *Mill.*
Edgew. Seikh Protected States, cultivated; Multan, cultivated.
A. Jhelum; Hushiarpur, cultivated.
J. L. S. Peshaur, uncommon, cultivated.
H. f. & T. Throughout India cultivated, but chiefly in the north.
In the Seikh States, according to Edgeworth, in some parts cultivated for the oil of the seeds only.

25. **P. cornigerum**, *Stocks.*
J. L. S. Peshaur.
H. f. & T. Punjab to Peshaur, *Vicary*; Afghan., *Griffith*; Beluch., *Stocks.*

26. **Argemone mexicana**, *L.*
Edgew. Amballa, not at Multan.
A. At Amritsur, Loodiana, Hushiarpur, but not at Jhelum; not mentioned as occurring at Peshaur by J. L. Stewart.
Stocks. Indus basin.
H. f. & T. Throughout the plains of India, most common; certainly introduced.

FUMARIACEÆ.

27. **Hypecoum procumbens**, *L.*
Edgew. Multan.
J. L. S. Peshaur.
H. f. & T. Punjab and Peshaur, *Vicary*; Salt-range, *Fleming*; Beluch., *Stocks*; Afghan., *Griffith.*

28. **Fumaria parviflora**, *Lam.*, var. **Vaillantii.**
Edgew. Multan.
A. Jhelum; Hushiarpur.
J. L. S. Peshaur.
T. T. Lahore.

CRUCIFERÆ.

29. **Nasturtium officinale**, *Br.*
A. Jhelum.
H. f. & T.—*Griffith*, Afghan.; *T. T.* Kashmir: doubt its being native.

30. N. terrestre, *Br.*
N. palustre, *DC.*
H. f. & T.—T. T. Punjab; Lahore.

31. N. indicum, *L.*
H. f. & T. Punjab.

32. N. montanum, *Wall.*
Edgew. Hajipur; Zilla Hushiarpur.
H. f. & T.—T. T. Punjab.

33. Arabis alpina, *Linn.*
Edgew. Hb., Fleming. Salt range, abundant.
H. f. & T. Western temperate Himalaya, 5000 to 11,000 ft., common.
Str. & Wint. Kumaon.
Jacq. Kashmir.
Fleming. Marri.

34. Cardamine hirsuta, *L.*
Edgew. Hajipur; Zilla Hushiarpur.
H. f. & T. In all temperate Himalaya, alt. 4000 to 12,000 ft., from Kashmir, *T. T.*, to Bhotan, *Griffith.*

35. Notoceras canariense, *Br.*
H. f. & T.—Vicary, Punjab to Peshaur; *Stocks,* Beluch.; *Griff.*, Afghan.
J. L. S. Peshaur (*Notoceras* species), perhaps this.
Edgew. Hb., J. Young. Attock.

36. Farsetia Edgeworthii, *H. f. & T.*
H. f. & T.—Fleming, Salt range; Punjab.
Edgew. Multan; Chandnot rocks.

37. F. Jacquemontii, *H. f. & T.*
Edgew. Multan; Lahore.
A. Jhelum.
H. f. & T.—Jacquemont, Punjab; Pind-Dadun-Khan; *T. T.*, Loodiana; *Fleming,* Salt range; *Dalzell,* Sindh; *Stocks,* Beluch.; *Griff.*, Afghan.

38. F. Hamiltonii, *Royle.*
Royle. From Delhi to Agra.
Edgew. Multan; Balanwali; Loodiana.
T. T. Lahore.
H. f. & T. Sup. Gangetic plain, between Agra and Delhi, *Wall.*; *T. T.*, Punjab.

39. Alyssum calycinum, *L.*
J. L. S. Peshaur, "not collected to the east of the Suliman range before."

40. COCHLEARIA FLAVA, *Ham.*
C. alyssoides, *DC.*
Edgew. Multan; Thanesar.
Royle. Northern India.
H. f. & T. Super. and infer. Gangetic plain, from the Soane to Moradabad.

41. MALCOLMIA AFRICANA, *Br.*
Arabis arvensis, *Edgew.*
Edgew. Multan; Lahore.
A. Jhelum.
J. L. S. Peshaur.
T. T. Ferozepur; Lahore.
H. f. & T. Punjab; *Griffith,* Afghan.; *Stocks,* Beluch.

42. M. STRIGOSA, *Boiss.*
A. Jhelum.
H. f. & T.—Fleming, Salt range, Punjab; *Vicary,* Peshaur; *Griff.,* Afghan.; *Stocks,* Beluch.
J. Young, Hb. Edgew. Attock.
J. L. S. Peshaur. "Pretty purple-lilac flowers; Europeans call it heather; as far east as Hassan-abdal."

43. SISYMBRIUM IRIO, *L.*
Edgew. Multan; cult. Ambala.
A. Jhelum; Hushiarpur.
J. L. S. Peshaur.
H. f. & T.—Jacquemont, Punjab; *Stocks,* Beluch.

44. S. IRIOIDES, *Boiss.*
Edgew. Multan; Sandal-Bar.
H. f. & T.—T. T. Punjab; *Griffith,* Afghan.; *Jacqt.,* Ajmir, cult.

45. S. SOPHIA, *L.*
A. Jhelum; Hushiarpur.
J. L. S. Peshaur.
H. f. & T.—Griffith, Afghan., 9000 to 10,000 ft.; *Stocks,* Beluch.

46. LEPTALEUM FILIFOLIUM, *DC.*
L. pygmæum, *DC.*
J. L. S. Peshaur.
H. f. & T.—Vicary, near Peshaur; *Stocks,* Beluch.; *Griff.,* Afghan.

47. BRASSICA CAMPESTRIS, *L.*
Sinapis dichotoma, *Roxb. Fl. Ind.*
S. glauca, *Roxb. Fl. Ind.*
Edgew. Seikh Protected States, called "Turia;" Multan, "Sarson."
A. Jhelum; Googerat; Hushiarpur, largely cultivated, "Surson."

J. L. S. Peshaur ("*Sinapis* is largely cultivated").

H. f. & T. "Throughout the whole of India, Himalaya, Beluch., Afghan., and Tibet cult. for its bland oil. Hind. 'Rai;' used for food by the natives, as well as for burning."

48. B. JUNCEA, *L.*

Edgew. Multan, cultiv., "Rai;" Mulana.

H. f. & T. "Cultiv. throughout all India, temperate and tropical Himalaya, Tibet, and Afghan. This is the 'Soorsa,' an acrid mustard, cultiv. for its oil, used for burning, rubbing the body in illness, &c."

49. B. NIGRA, *Koch.*

Sinapis erysimoides, *Roxb.*

H. f. & T.—*Griff.*, Afghan.; *Stocks*, Beluch.; *T. T.* Kunawar. Common mustard, rarely cultiv. in India.

50. B. ERUCA, *L.*

Edgew. Seikh Protected States, called "Sarson;" Multan.

A. Jhelum; Hushiarpur, cultiv., called also "Surson."

H. f. & T.—*Str. & Wint.*, in western temperate Himalaya; *T. T.* Superior Gangetic plain and Punjab; *Griff.*, Afghanistan, 10,000 to 12,000 ft.

A. Yields an oil very similar to that of *B. campestris*, and used in exactly the same way, and called the same by the natives.

51. B. STOCKSII, *H. f. & T.*

Edgew. Multan, not cultivated; Jhung.

H. f. & T.—*Stocks*, Beluchistan; *Edgeworth & T. T.*, Punjab and western temperate Tibet; *Jacq.*, from Delhi to Ajmir.

52. B. GRIFFITHII, *H. f. & T.*

H. f. & T.—*Fleming*, Punjab, Kala-bag Salt range; *Stocks*, Beluchistan; *Griffith*, Afghan.

53. B. RAPA, *L.*

Edgew. Multan, cult.

54. MORICANDIA TORTUOSA, *H. f. & T.*

Douepia tortuosa, *Camb.*

H. f. & T.—*Fleming*, Salt range; *Jacq.*, Punjab, near Pind-Dadun-Khan.

55. CAPSELLA BURSA-PASTORIS, *L.*

A. Jhelum; Hushiarpur; Umritsur.

J. L. S. Peshaur.

H. f. & T.—*Griffith*, Afghan.; *Stocks*, Beluch.

56. LEPIDIUM DRABA, *L.*

J. L. S. Peshaur.

H. f. & T.—*Vicary*, Peshaur; *Stocks*, Beluch.; *Griff.*, Afghan.

57. L. SATIVUM, *L.*

Edgew. Multan, cult.; Amballa, garden.

A. Jhelum, an escape, also cultivated.

58. L. ruderale, *L.*

J. L. S. Peshaur.

H. f. & T. In western temperate Tibet, alt. 7000 to 13,000 ft.; *Griffith*, Afghan.

59. Dipterygium glaucum, *Dcn.*

Isatis spartioides, *Edgew.*

Edgew. Punjab; Multan; sand-hills between Beeas and Sutlej.

60. Neslia paniculata, *Desv.*

J. L. S. Peshaur, not collected before to the east of the Suliman range.

H. f. & T.—*T. T.*, in western temperate Himalaya and Kashmir, 5000 to 6000 ft.; *Stocks*, Beluch., frequent; *Griffith*, Afghan.

61. Euclidium syriacum, *Br.*

J. L. S. Peshaur; "not collected before to the east of Suliman range."

H. f. & T.—*T. T. and Winterbottom*, western temperate Himalaya and Kashmir, 5000 to 6000 ft.; *Griffith*, Afghan., frequent.

62. Physorhynchus Brahuicus, *Stocks.*

A. Jhelum and Salt range.

Stocks. Sindh.

63. Raphanus sativus, *L.*

Edgew. Multan, cult.; Amballa, cult., "Muli."

H. f. & T. Cult. throughout India, temperate Himalaya, Tibet, Afghan.

64. R. raphanistrum, *DC.*

Edgew. Seikh Protected States, cultivated, both for the oil from the seeds, as well as for the pods used as a vegetable.

A. A common Punjab garden vegetable.

The oil in the Seikh States called "Tárá-mira."

65. Goldbachia lævigata, *DC.*

Edgew. Multan.

A. Jhelum.

J. L. S. Peshaur.

T. T. Lahore.

H. f. & T.— *T. T.*, *Jacq.*, Punjab, frequent; *Stocks*, Beluch.; *Griff.*, Afghan.

66. Chorispora, sp.

J. L. S. Peshaur.

CAPPARIDACEÆ.

67. Polanisia viscosa, *Wall.*

P. icosandra, *W. & A.*

Edgew. Ferozepur; Multan.

T. T. Lahore.

A. Jhelum.
J. L. S. Peshaur.
Stocks. Sindh.
Griff. Afghan.

68. GYNANDROPSIS PENTAPHYLLA, *DC.*
Edgew. Multan; Chandnot.
T. T. Lahore.
Jacq. Delhi; Ajmir.
A. Jhelum; Hushiarpur.

69. CLEOME DROSERÆFOLIA, *Delil.*
J. L. S. Peshaur.

70. C. LINEARIS, *Stocks.*
C. papillosa, *Steud.*
C. gracilis, *Edgew.*
C. leptocarpa, *Stocks.*
Edgew. Multan; Sandal Bar.
A. Jhelum.
J. L. S. Peshaur.
Vicary. Boogta Hills.
Stocks. Sindh; Beluch.

71. C. PENTANERVIA, *DC.*
Stocks. Sindh, lower hills.

72. C. RUTA, *Camb.*
C. brachycarpa, *DC.* (*Edgew.*).
Edgew. Sandal Bar; Multan; Loodiana.
T. T. Lahore.
Jacq. Pind-Dadun-Khan.
A. Jhelum.
J. L. S. Peshaur.
Vicary. Boogta Hills.
Stocks. Sindh.

73. C. STOCKSIANA, *Boiss.*
Vicary. Boogta Hills; Sindh.
Stocks. Upper and Lower Beluchistan.

74. C. VAHLIANA, *Fresn.*
Stocks. Sindh.

75. CRATÆVA RELIGIOSA, *L.*
C. Roxburghii, *Br.*
Edgew. Sewaliks, wild; Amballa, planted near towns; Multan.
T. T. Cult. Meerut; Lahore; Seharanpur.
A. Indigenous Jhelum and Hushiarpur Hills, also cult.
J. L. S. Not at Peshaur.

76. CADABA FARINOSA, *Forsk.*
C. Indica, *Lam.*
Edgew. Multan.
Stocks. Sindh.

77. C. HETEROTRICHA, *Stocks.*
Stocks. Sindh.

78. SODADA DECIDUA, *Forsk.*
Capparis aphylla, *Roxb.*
C. sodada, *Br.*
C. decidua.
Edgew. Amballa; Seikh Protected States; Multan.
T. T. Lahore; east of Ferozepur; its eastern limit Sirhind.
A. Jhelum; Hushiarpur.
J. L. S. Peshaur.
Stocks. Indus basin (the sandy plains of Sindh through which the Indus river flows).

79. CAPPARIS HORRIDA, *L.*
Edgew. Sadhaura.
T. T. Seharanpur; Moradabad.
Jacq. Dehra-Dhun.
A. Hushiarpur, Philur, very common in jungle. "Hees," utilized for hedges.

80. C. SEPIARIA, *L.*
Edgew. Amballa; Seikh Protected States; Pinjor-Dhūn (var. *subinermis*).
T. T. Loodiana; Meerut; Moradabad.
Edgew. Seikh States; native name "Hins."

81. C. SPINOSA, *L.*
C. obovata, *Royle.*
Edgew. Multan; Kulu Himalaya, 6000 ft.
T. T. Sutlej valley to 3500 ft.
Jacq. Kumaon.
A. Jhelum; Salt range; Hushiarpur; rocks at Rupur.
Fleming. Salt range.
J. L. S. Peshaur.
Vicary. Peshaur.
Stocks. Sindh.

82. C. SPINOSA, *L.*, var. GALEATA, *Stocks.*
Stocks. Kurrachee.
Vicary. Beluch. and Lower Kurrachee.
Griffith. Afghan.

83. C. SPINOSA, L., var. PARVIFLORA, *Boiss.*
Edgew. Multan.
Stocks. Sindh Hills.
Griff. Afghan.

84. NIEBUHRIA LINEARIS, *Stocks, DC.*
N. oblongifolia, *DC.*
Royle. Near Delhi.
T. T. Delhi.
Stocks. Indus basin.

RESEDACEÆ.

85. OCHRADENUS BACCATUS, *Delil.*
Vicary. Sindh.
Stocks. Sindh; Indus basin.
Griff. Afghan.

86. OLIGOMERIS GLAUCESCENS, *Camb.*
Reseda oligandra, *Edgew.*
Edgew. Loodiana; Multan.
T. T. Lahore to Delhi; Karnál; Ferozepur.
Jacq. Loodiana.
A. Jhelum; Hushiarpur.
Fleming. Salt range.
J. L. S. Peshaur.
Stocks. Sindh; Beluch.
Griff. Afghan.

87. RESEDA BRACTEATA, *Boiss.*
Fleming. Salt range.
Stocks. Beluch.
Griff. Afghan.

88. R. AUCHERI, *Boiss.*
Stocks. Sindh.

VIOLARIEÆ.

89. VIOLA CANESCENS, *Wall.*
T. T. Jamu hills; Chamba.

90. V. CINEREA, *Boiss.*
T. T. Banks of Chenab.
Jacq. Delhi to Ajmir.
A. Jhelum.
Fleming. Salt range.
J. Young, Hb. Edgew. Attock.
Vicary. Boogta Hills.
Stocks. Sindh.
Griffith. Afghan.

91. V. PATRINII, *DC.*
J. L. S. Peshaur?

92. V. SERPENS, *Wall.*
Edgew. Kūlū.
Madden. Garwhal.
A. Hushiarpur.

93. V. TRICOLOR, *L.*
A. Jhelum, an escape, common garden weed.

94. IONIDIUM SUFFRUTICOSUM, *Ging.*
Royle. Gangetic valley, nearly as far as Delhi.
Jameson. Agra.

BIXINEÆ.

95. FLACOURTIA SAPIDA, *Roxb.*
Royle. North-west provinces.
Edgew. Khizerabad; Jagadhri.
T. T. Moradabad; Meerut; Loodiana; Jamu Hills.
A. Jhelum; Hushiarpur.
Stocks. Sha-Bilawal; Beluchistan to Kurrachee.
Royle states, "the fruit small, of a pleasant sweetish flavour."
A. At Hushiarpur called "Kăngoo."

96. XYLOSMA LONGIFOLIUM, *Clos.*
T. T. Jamu.
A. Hushiarpur, called "Thukola;" common in Gūgrate jungle.
J. L. S. Rajaori (Ganges); Marri.

PITTOSPOREÆ.

97. PITTOSPORUM FLORIBUNDUM, *W. & A.*
Senacia nepalensis, *DC.*
T. T. Petora.
St. & Wint. 1500 feet, Kumaon.
Jacq. No. 1014.

POLYGALEÆ.

98. POLYGALA TRIFLORA, *W. & A., an L.?*
Edgeworth. Loodiana.
A. Jhelum.
J. L. S. Peshaur.
T. T. Lahore, between Delhi and Karnál.

Var. GRANDIFLORA, *Wall.*
Edgew. Amballa.

Var. HYDASPICA, *Edgew.*
P. erioptera, *DC.*
P. blepharidium, *Edgw.*
Edgew. Multan.

99. P. ARVENSIS, *Willd.*
T. T. Moradabad; Dehra-Dhūn; Rechnab-Doab; Jamu; Lahore; Delhi to Karnal.
Vicary. Punjab.
Jacq. Rajaori.
A. Jhelum.

100. P. GERARDIANA, *Wall.*
Edgew. Multan.
T. T. Punjab; Jamu Hills.
Vicary. Peshaur.

101. P. HOHENACKERIANA, *F. & M.*
Vicary. Attock.
Stocks. Beluchistan.

102. P. TELEPHIOIDES, *Willd.*
Royle. Delhi.

FRANKENIACEÆ.

103. FRANKENIA PULVERULENTA, *L.*
Edgew. Multan.
T. T. Lahore.
J. L. S. Peshaur.
Vicary. Peshaur.
Griffith. Afghan.

CARYOPHYLLEÆ.

104. DIANTHUS CRINITUS, *Sm.*
A. Jhelum (not in 'Flora of Jhelum').
Fleming. Salt range.
J. L. S. Peshaur.
Vicary. Peshaur.
Stocks. Beluchistan.
Griffith. Afghan.

105. **VACCARIA PARVIFLORA,** ***Mœnch.***
Gypsophila vaccaria, *Sib.*
Edgew. Radaur; Multan.
T. T. Meerut; Moradabad; Jamu; Ferozepur; Loodiana; Lahore.
A. Jhelum; Umritsur.
Stocks. Sindh.

106. **SILENE APETALA,** ***L.***
Vicary. Peshaur.

107. **S. CONOIDEA,** ***L.***
S. conica, *L.*
Edgew. Sadhaura; Multan.
T. T. Moradabad; Punjab; Lahore; Ladak, 11,000 ft.
Jacq. Delhi; Loodiana.
A. Jhelum; Hushiarpur; Umritsur.
J. L. S. Peshaur.
Stocks. Beluchistan.
Griffith. Afghan.

108. **S. LEYSEROIDES,** ***Boiss.***
J. Young, Hb. Edgew. Attock.
J. L. S. Peshaur.
Vicary. Peshaur.
Griffith. Afghan.

109. **S. RUBELLA,** ***L.***
A. Jhelum, escape, garden weed.

110. **ALSINE FASCICULATA,** ***Stocks.***
Vicary. Peshaur.
Stocks. Sindh; Beluch.

111. **ARENARIA GLOBULOSA,** ***Labil.***
J. L. S. Peshaur.

112. **A. SERPYLLIFOLIA,** ***L.***
A. muralis, *Edgew.*
Edgew. Thanesar; Khizerabad.
T. T. Jamu; Ferozepur; Loodiana.
A. Jhelum; Hushiarpur.
J. L. S. Peshaur.
Griffith. Afghan.

113. **STELLARIA MEDIA,** ***L.***
Edgew. Multan.
T. T. Loodiana; Lahore.
A. Jhelum (not in 'Flora of Jhelum').
J. L. S. Peshaur.

114. MALACHIUM AQUATICUM, *Fries.*
T. T. Jamu.
Jacq. Punjab.

115. SPERGULARIA PENTANDRA, *L.*
Edgew. Multan.
T. T. Moradabad; Sirhind; Ferozepur; Loodiana; Lahore.
Jacq. Punjab.
J. L. S. Peshaur.
Stocks. No. 595.

116. S. RUBRA, *Pers.*
Arenaria flaccida, *Roxb.*
A. rubra, *L.*
Edgew. Multan; Jhung; Meerut; Amballa.
T. T. Lahore.
A. Jhelum; Hushiarpur.
J. L. S. Peshaur.
Stocks. No. 788.
Griffith. Afghan.

117. HAPALOSIA LŒFLINGIÆ, *Wall.*
T. T. Moradabad.
Edgew. Banda.

118. LŒFLINGIA, sp.
Vicary. Peshaur.

119. POLYCARPÆA CORYMBOSA, *Lam.*
P. spadicea, *Lam.*
Edgew. Multan.
T. T. Rohilkhand; Moradabad; Sirindh; Loodiana; Lahore.
Jacq.
A. Jhelum; Hushiarpur.
Stocks. Indus basin.

PORTULACEÆ.

120. PORTULACA OLERACEA, *L.*
Edgew. Umballa; Multan.
T. T. Moradabad; Delhi; Lahore.
Jacqt. (Punjab?)
A. Jhelum; Hushiarpur; Umritsur.
J. L. S. Peshaur.
Griffith. Afghan.
A. Commonly cultivated throughout the Punjab, as a pot-herb. Jhelum, called "Monka."

121. P. QUADRIFIDA, *L.*
P. geniculata, *Hb. Royle.*
P. meridiana, *L. fil.*
Edgew. Multan, indigenous and cult.
T. T. Moradabad; Delhi; Loodiana; Lahore.
Jacq. No. 1543.
J. L. S. Peshaur.
A. Jhelum. Cultivated in the Punjab.
Stocks. No. 17. Indus basin.

122. P. TUBEROSA, *Roxb.*
Stocks. No. 445. Indus basin; Kurrachee.

123. TALINUM CUNEIFOLIUM, *Willd.*
Stocks. No. 610. Beluchistan to Kurrachee.

TAMARISCINEÆ.

124. TAMARIX ARTICULATA, *Vahl.*
T. orientalis, *Forsk.*
Royle. Delhi.
Edgew. Seikh Protected States; Multan; Amballa.
T. T. Sutlej provinces.
A. Sindh; Multan; Jhelum (in 'Flora' only probably).
J. L. S. Peshaur (doubtful if indigenous).
Falconer. Punjab.
Stocks. Sindh; Indus basin.
Cultivated as well as indigenous in the Punjab, *T. T.*, *Edgew.*, *A.* Perhaps not indigenous, but only cult., Peshaur, *J. L. S.*
Multan and Seikh Protected States, called "Fras," "Pharma," *Edgew.*
Sindh, *A.*, "Asree-loua."

125. T. DIOICA, *Roxb.*
Royle. North-western India.
Edgew. Banks of Ravee-Multan.
T. T. Everywhere, Moradabad; Lahore.
A. Jhelum; Sindh; Hushiarpur; Beas. Sindh, "Pilchee."
J. L. S. Peshaur.
Stocks. Indus basin.
Griffith. Afghan.

126. T. GALLICA, *L.*
T. indica, *Willd.*
Royle. Jumna.
Edgew. Punjab; Multan.

T. T. Lahore; Ferozepur.
A. Jhelum; Hushiarpur; Sindh, "Laee."
J. L. S. Peshaur.
Griffith. Afghan.
A. Is also cultivated in Jhelum and Hushiarpur; *J. L. S.* cult. Peshaur.

Var. PALLASII.
Sindh, *Stocks.*
T. T. Tibet; Nubra.

127. TAMARIX.
Trichaurus auchenaiacus, *Decais.*
Fleming. West bank of Indus.

128. REAUMURIA VERMICULATA, *L.*
Stocks. Beluch.

ELATINEÆ.

129. BERGIA AMMANIOIDES, *Roxb.*
Edgew. Multan; Loodiana.
T. T. Moradabad; Meerut; Lahore.
J. L. S. Peshaur.
Griffith. Afghan.

130. B. SUFFRUTICOSA, *Fenzl.*
Lancretia suffruticosa, *Del.*
Elatine æstivosa, *W. & A.*
E. fragrans, *Edgew.*
Royle. North-west India.
Edgew. Multan; Balanwali.
T. T. Loodiana, Ferozepur; Lahore.
J. L. S. Peshaur.
Vicary. Punjab.

131. B. VERTICILLATA, *Willd.*
Royle. Is found in India as well as in Egypt.

GUTTIFERÆ.

132. XANTHOCHYMUS PICTORIUS, *Roxb.*
Royle. Cultivated at Delhi, called "Dephul." A very southern tree.

TERNSTRŒMIACEÆ.

133. THEA, species.
A. Tea. Cultivated in the Purwain range, Hushiarpur district, also Kangra valley.

DIPTEROCARPACEÆ.

134. SHOREA ROBUSTA, *Roxb.*
T. T. Kumaon.
St. & W. Kumaon, 2000 ft.
A. Hushiarpur, in a natural forest, its western limit: native name "Saul." I have never seen any, except seedlings, as cultivated trees.

MALVACEÆ.

135. ALTHÆA LUDWIGII, L.
Malva Malwensis, *Edgew.*
Edgew. Hureppa; Balanwali; Multan; Banda.
T. T. Punjab; Ferozepur.
Vicary. Sindh.
Stocks. Sindh; Beluchistan.

136. MALVA PARVIFLORA, *L.*
Edgew. Multan.
T. T. Moradabad; Jamu; Ferozepur; Loodiana; Lahore.
A. Jhelum; Hushiarpur.
J. L. S. Peshaur.
Stocks. Sindh.

137. M. SYLVESTRIS, *L.*
Royle. Hort.
T. T. Lahore; Kumaon; Kashmir.
Jacq. No. 908.
A. Hushiarpur, a common garden-weed.

138. M. VULGARIS, *Fries.*
M. rotundifolia, *Cav.* non *L.*
Edgew. Multan.
T. T. Lahore; Kumaon.
Fleming. Marri.
Stocks. Sindh.

139. SIDA CORDIFOLIA, *L.*
Edgew. Multan; Loodiana.
T. T. Moradabad; Punjab; Chenab; Rampur.
Jacq. Rajaori.
A. Jhelum.

140. S. GREWIOIDES, *A. Rich.*
Edgew. Multan; Punjab.
Stocks. Sindh.

141. S. HUMILIS, *Willd.*
Edgew. Multan.
T. T. Bari-Doab; Lahore; Punjab; Dehra-Dhun; Moradabad.
Jacq. Punjab; Himalaya.
A. Jhelum.

142. S. RHOMBIFOLIA, *L.*
Edgew. Amballa; Thanesar.
T. T. Lahore; Punjab; Moradabad.
Jacq. Punjab; Delhi to Bijnore; Rajaori.
A. Jhelum.
Fleming. Salt range.

143. S. SPINOSA, *L.*
S. alba, *L.*
T. T. Meerut; Lahore.
Vicary. Sindh.
Stocks. Sindh.

144. ABUTILON BIDENTATUM, *Planch.*
Stocks. Sindh.
Edgew. Loodiana.
T. T. Punjab; Lahore.

145. A. GRAVEOLENS, *W. & A.*
Jacq. Kumaon.
Vicary. Sindh.
Stocks. Beluch.

146. A. INDICUM, *G. Don.*
Edgew. Multan.
T. T. Moradabad; Lahore.
Jacq. Delhi.
A. Jhelum; Hushiarpur.
J. L. S. Peshaur.
Stocks. Indus-basin.

146*. A. MUTICUM, *G. Don.*
A. tomentosa, *W. & A.*
Edgew. Multan.
Stocks. Indus basin.
Griffith. Afghan.

147. URENA LOBATA, *L.*
T. T. Moradabad.
Jacq. Rajaori.
A. Hushiarpur.

148. U. REPANDA, *Roxb.*
Royle. North-west India.
T. T. Moradabad, jungles near the hills; Rechnab-Doab.
Falconer. Upper Gangetic plain.

149. Pavonia.
Hibiscus microphyllus, *Vahl.*
Stocks. Sindh.
Vicary. Kurrachee.

150. P. odorata, *Willd.*
Edgew. Banda.
Stocks. Indus basin; Sindh.

151. Pavonia.
Lebretonia procumbens, *W. & A.*
Stocks. Sindh.

152. P. zeylanica, *Cav.*
Stocks. Sindh; Indus basin.

153. Hibiscus Abelmoschus, *L.*
Abelmoschus moschatus, *W. & A.*
Royle. Banks of the Jumna. "Mucilage of the seeds employed in clarifying sugar" in the Seharanpur district. "Hub-ool-mushk," "musk-scented seeds."

156. H. cannabinus, *L.*
Edgew. Seikh Protected States, cult.
T. T. Cultivated, Moradabad; Lahore; Punjab.
Jacq. Punjab, cultivated.
A. Jhelum; Umritsur, cultivated usually in strips round fields.
Edgew. Seikh States, "San."
Royle. "Sun."

157. Hibiscus.
Abelmoschus ficulneus, *L.*
T. T. Jamu; Punjab plains.
J. *L. S.* Peshaur.

158. H. Gibsonii, *Stocks.*
Royle. North-west India.
A. Jhelum.
Stocks. Sindh.
Griffith. Afghan.

159. H. hirtus, *L.* (non *Cav.*).
Edgew. Pinjor-Dhun, indigenous.
T. T. Moradabad.
Jacq. Hedges, Seharanpur.
J. L. S. Peshaur.

160. H. laguneoides, *Edgew.*
Edgew. Multan; Madhapur.
Stocks. Sindh.

161. H. LONGIFOLIUS, *Willd.*
Abelmoschus esculentus, *W. & A.*
Royle. North-west India, cultivated.
A. Jhelum, cultivated.
Edgew. Multan; Sirindh (also a dissected-leaved form), cultivated: called "Bhindi," "Ram-turai."
Royle. "Ram-turai."

162. H. MACROPHYLLUS, *Roxb.*
T. T. Moradabad.
Griffith. Terrai; Kashia.

163. H. MICRANTHUS, *L. fil.*
Royle. Delhi (*rigidus*, β).
Edgew. Multan.
T. T. Near Delhi.

164. H. MUTABILIS, *L.*
Edgew. Cultivated, Amballa.
T. T. Lahore; Moradabad, cult.

165. HIBISCUS.
Abelmoschus racemosus, *Wall.*
H. cancellatus, *Roxb.*
Royle. Jumna, north lat. 31°.
Edgew. Pinjor-Dhun.
Blink. Kumaon, 4000 feet.

166. H. RIGIDUS, *L. fil.*
Royle. Delhi.

167. H. SCINDICUS, *Stocks.*
Stocks. Sindh, No. 480.

168. H. SABDARIFFA, *L.*
Royle. Cult. North-west India.
A. Cult. throughout the Punjab gardens; native name "Putwa." Does not ripen its seed, owing to the frost.

169. H. SURATTENSIS, *L.*
Royle. Delhi.
(This is a Bengal, Prome, and Rangoon plant, *H. f. & T.*) Royle's may not be this plant, but *H. furcatus*, Roxb.

170. H. TRIONUM, *L.*
T. T. Hort. Moradabad.
Stocks. Sindh.
Griffith. Afghan.

171. H. VITIFOLIUS, *L.*
T. T. Moradabad.
Jacq. Rajaori.
A. Jhelum.

172. **Decaschistia crotonifolia**, *W. & A.*
Royle. Delhi.

173. **Gossypium herbaceum**, *L.*
Edgew. Seikh States; ruins at Thanesar (var. *arboreum*), *Hb. Edgew.*; Multan.
T. T. Lahore; Moradabad.
A. Jhelum; Hushiarpur (var. *arboreum*, cult.).
J. L. S. Peshaur.
Stocks. Beluch. to Kurrachee.
A. Cultivated throughout the Punjab; and in some places the variety *arboreum* has been introduced. The cotton as a rule is poor. Called "Kupas."

174. **Lagunea lobata**, *Willd.*
Edgew. Pinjor-Dhun.
T. T. Bijnore.
A. Jhelum.

175. **Bombax heptaphyllum**, *L.*
T. T. Moradabad, a forest-tree, never far out into the plains.
A. Jhelum, Mt. Tilla, and Salt range; Hushiarpur jungles, common. A large tree in the forests. Called "Sembul" and "Semul." Frequently cultivated in the plains. "Cotton-tree."

176. **Kydia calycina**, *Roxb.*
T. T. Forest-tree, Moradabad; Jamu hills.
Jacq. Rajaori, No. 943.
A. Jhelum; Mt. Tilla; Hushiarpur hills. The bark used at Hushiarpur for clarifying sugar.

177. **Serræa incana**, *Cav.*
Stocks. Sindh rocks.
Vicary. Kurrachee.

STERCULIACEÆ.

178. **Sterculia**, sp.
A. Jhelum; Mt. Tilla.

179. **Helicteres Isora**, *L.*
T. T. Jamu.
St. & W. Kumaon, 1000 ft.

180. **Pentapetes phœnicia**, *L.*
Edgew. Cult. Amballa (*coccinea*, Hb. Edgew.).
T. T. Upper Punjab; hort. Moradabad.

181. **Melhania abutiloides**, *Arn.*
M. Bandelhana, *Edgew.*
Royle. North-west India.
Falconer. Delhi.

A. Jhelum.
J. L. S. Peshaur.
Stocks. Deesa, Beluchistan to Kurrachee.

182. M. OVATA.
Brotera ovata, *Cav.*
H. f. & T.—Stocks, Sindh.

183. M. SIDÆFOLIA, *Stocks.*
Stocks. Sindh, No. 536.

184. ABROMA AUGUSTA, *L. fil.*
Edgew. Hort. Amballa.
T. T. Hort. Seharanpur.

TILIACEÆ.

185. CORCHORUS ACUTANGULUS, *Lam.*
Edgew. Amballa.
T. T. Lahore; Kalka.
A. Jhelum; Hushiarpur.
Stocks. Indus basin.

186. C. CAPSULARIS, *L.*
Royle. Cult. in Bengal.
Edgew. Thanesar, Multan.
T. T. Moradabad; Lahore.
Royle. "Its fibres, with those of *C. olitorius*, are cultivated in Bengal, and called "Jute" or "Pat," of which gummy bags are made."

187. CORCHORUS.
Antichorus depressus, *L. fil.*
Edgew. Multan.
T. T. Lahore.
Stocks. Sindh.
Griff. Afghan.
Royle. Delhi (as *C. postratus*).

188. C. FASCICULARIS, *Lam.*
Royle. Delhi.
Edgew. Multan; Muk-dūn-pūr jungle.
Stocks. Indus basin; Sindh.

189. C. OLITORIUS, *L.*
Edgew. Amballa.
T. T. Moradabad; Lahore; Rampur.
Jacq. Dehra-Dhun; Agra.
A. Jhelum; Hushiarpur.
J. L. S. Peshaur.
Griffith. Afghan.

190. C. TRIDENS, *L.*
Royle. Delhi (as *C. linearis*); North-west India.
Edgew. Amballa.
T. T. Lahore.
A. Jhelum; Hushiarpur.
Stocks. Sindh; Indus basin.

191. C. TRILOCULARIS, *L.*
Edgew. Multan; Amballa.
T. T. Delhi; Amballa; Lahore; plains below Jamu.
Jacq. Pind-Dadun-Khan, No. 962.
J. L. S. Peshaur.
Stocks. Indus basin.
Royle. (Royle herb. *C. humilis* is *C. trilocularis*, L.); Delhi; North-west India.

192. TRIUMFETTA ANGULATA, *Lam.*
T. T. Rampur; Moradabad.
Jacq. Rajaori.
A. Jhelum.

193. T. ANNUA, *L.*
T. T. Kalka; Simla.

194. T. NEGLECTA, *W. & A.*
T. T. Moradabad.

195. T. PILOSA, *Roth.*
T. T. Dehra-Dhun.

196. T. ROTUNDIFOLIA, *Lam.*
Edgew. Multan.
Stocks. Indus basin.

197. GREWIA ASIATICA, *L.*
Edgew. Cult. Multan.
T. T. Rowlee-Ghat, indigenous. The wild plant quite similar to the garden one; hort. Lahore; Moradabad; Seharanpur.
A. Hushiarpur indigenous, and hort. Umritsur.
J. L. S. Not at Peshaur.
A. Cultivated throughout the Punjab for its "pleasant acid berry." "Phalsa."

198. G. BETULÆFOLIA, *Juss.*
G. populifolia, *Vahl.*
Edgew. Chandnot Rocks; Sandal Bar; Multan.
T. T. Jamu.
Jacq. Punjab; Phagwara.
A. Jhelum.
J. L. S. Peshaur.
Vicary. Boogta Hills.
Stocks. Sindh.

199. G. HELICTERIFOLIA, *Wall.*
G. polygama, *Roxb.*
Edgew. Radaur, amongst *Butea.* (Edgeworth considers his plants to be *G. polygama,* Roxb., and that this is perhaps the same as *G. helicterifolia,* Wall. On examination this seems to be the case; at least Edgeworth's plant marked *G. polygama,* Roxb., is apparently *G. helicterifolia,* Wall.)
Royle. North-west India.
J. L. S., Hb. G. Henderson. Salt range.

200. G. HIRSUTA, *Vahl.*
T. T. Rowlee-Ghat.

201. G. OPPOSITIFOLIA, *Benth.*
T. T. Punjab, foot of hills; Jamu Hills.
A. Jhelum; Hushiarpur.
Fleming. Salt range.
J. L. S. Peshaur.
A. Hushiarpur; called "Bahur" and "Bahul."
J. L. S. The "Daman" of the Punjab.

202. G. ORIENTALIS, *L.*
T. T. Banks of the Chenab.

203. G. RIGIDA, *Stocks.*
Stocks. Sindh Hills, from Beluchistan to Kurrachee.

204. G. ROTHII, *DC.*
G. bicolor, *Juss.*
A. Jhelum; Mt. Tilla.
J. L. S. Peshaur.
Stocks. Sindh, No. 532.

205. G. VILLOSA, *Roth.*
A. Jhelum.

LINEÆ.

206. LINUM STRICTUM, *L.*
T. T. Hot valleys, Jamu.
J. L. S. Peshaur.
Vicary. Peshaur.
Jacq. No. 1570 (183').
Griffith. Afghan.

207. L. USITATISSIMUM, *L.*
Edgew. Seikh States, cult.
T. T. Cultivated, Moradabad; Rajpur; Lahore.
A. Jhelum; Hushiarpur.
J. L. S. Peshaur, cult.
A. In all the above localities cultivated for its seed; at Sealkote and Kangra valley for its fibre, "Flax."

208. **Reinwardtia trigyna**, *Blanch.*
Linum trigynum, *Roxb.*
T. T. Moradabad, near the hills.
Jacq. No. 1606 (27").
J. L. S. Peshaur.

209. **R. repens**, *Don.*
T. T. Jamu; Simla.
St. & W. Kumaon, 2500 feet.

MALPIGHIACEÆ.

210. **Aspidopterys nutans**, *A. Juss.*
Hiræa nutans, *Roxb.*
H. lanuginosa, *Wall.*
Royle. Extends from the peninsula to the foot of the hills, Dehra-Dhun.
T. T. Garwhal.
St. & W. Kumaon, 4000 ft.

211. **Hiptage Madablota**, *Gaert.*
T. T. Jamu; Kumaon.
A. Hushiarpur.
St. & W. Kumaon, 1500 ft.

ZYGOPHYLLEÆ.

212. **Tribulus alatus**, *Delile.*
Edgew. Multan; Jhung.
Vicary. Sindh.
Stocks. Indus basin.

213. **T. terrestris**, *L.*
H. f. & T. (*T. lanuginosus* of Indian botanists.)
Royle. Northern India.
Edgew. Multan.
T. T. Everywhere in the plains of India; Moradabad; Karnál; Ferozepur; Loodiana; Jalinder; Lahore.
A. Jhelum; Hushiarpur.
Fleming. Salt range.
J. L. S. Peshaur.
Stocks. Sindh.
Griffith. Afghan.

214. **Seetzenia orientalis**, *Br.*
Vicary. Sindh.
Stocks. Sindh.

215. ZYGOPHYLLUM COCCINEUM, *L.*
Stocks. Sindh (is *Z. album* of Stocks's list).

216. Z. SIMPLEX, *L.*
Edgew. Multan; Sandal Bar.
Stocks. Sindh.
Vicary. Sindh.

217. FAGONIA CRETICA, *L.*
F. mysorensis, *Roth.*
F. arabica, *L.*
Royle. Delhi.
Edgew. Multan; Balanwali; Chandnot.
T. T. Punjab; Ferozepur; Loodiana; Jalinder; Lahore.
Fleming. Salt range.
A. Jhelum.
J. L. S. Peshaur.
Vicary. Peshaur; Lahore; Ferozepur; Sindh.
Stocks. Sindh.
Griffith. Afghan.

GERANIACEÆ.

218. GERANIUM OCELLATUM, *Camb.*
Edgew. Paota.
T. T. Jamu; Kumaon.
Str. & Wint. 1000–6000 ft., Kumaon.
Fleming. Salt range.
A. Jhelum; Mt. Tilla (and not *lucidum*, as in 'Flora of Jhelum'); Hushiarpur.

219. G. ROTUNDIFOLIUM, *L.*
Edgew. Jaswan-Dhun.
T. T. Jamu.
A. Jhelum; Mt. Tilla; Hushiarpur.
Stocks. Beluch.
Griffith. Afghan.

220. MONSONIA LAWIANA, *Stocks.*
Stocks. Beluchistan to Kurrachee.

221. M. MALLICA, *Edgew.*, near E. NIVEUM, *Decais.*
Edgew. Multan.
Vicary. Sindh.

222. ERODIUM CICUTARIUM, *L.*
St. & Wint. Simla hills.
J. L. S. Peshaur.
Vicary. Peshaur.
Griffith. Afghan.
Stocks. Beluchistan.

223. E. MARITIMUM, *L.*
J. L. S. Peshaur.

224. E. PULVERULENTUM, *Willd.*
Geranium pulverulentum, *Cav.*
Stocks. Beluch. inferior (*Hb. Edgew.*, no. 737).
J. Young. Attock, *Hb. Edgew.* no. 1248.

225. OXALIS ACETOSELLA, *L.*
T. T. Jamu, 8000 feet.
Fleming. Mt. Tilla (*Hb. Edgew.* no. 1429).

226. O. CORNICULATA, *L.*
Royle. North-west Provinces.
Edgew. Multan; from Calcutta to Punjab-Himalaya to 8000 feet.
T. T. Jamu; Punjab; Lahore.
A. Jhelum; Hushiarpur.
J. L. S. Peshaur.
Stocks. Sindh.
Griff. Afghan.

227. AVERRHOA CARAMBOLA, *L.*
Edgew. Jagadhri hort.
A. Hort. Jhelum; Hushiarpur, a large tree. Fruit called "Kumruck;" two varieties, a red and yellow. An uncommon fruit-tree in the Punjab.

RUTACEÆ.

228. LIMONIA ACIDISSIMA, *L.*
L. crenulata, *Roxb.*
Royle. Sutlej.
Edgew. Near Asafgurh.
T. T. Kalka.
A. Hushiarpur.
Edgew. Native name "Kynth."

229. GLYCOSMIS PENTAPHYLLA, *Correa.*
Royle. Sutlej.
T. T. Rohilkhand; Seharanpur.
Jacq. Rohilkhand; Seharanpur.
St. & Wint. Kumaon, 2000 ft.

230. MURRAYA EXOTICA, *L.*
Edgew. Kalesar-Dhun.
T. T. Dehra-Dhun.
A. Hushiarpur, a common jungle-shrub, called "Nur-gung;" flowers in December.

231. M. Königii, *Oliv.*
Bergera Königii, *L.*
Edgew. Kalesar-Dhun.
T. T. Kumaon, 1000 ft.; Moradabad.
A. Hushiarpur, jungle-shrub, very common, called "Gandla."

232. Clausena Wampi, *Blanc.*
Cookia punctata, *Retz.*
T. T. Hort. Moradabad.
A. Hort. Hushiarpur, produces fruit freely. The "Wampi."

233. Feronia elephantum, *Roxb.*
A. Jhelum; Pind-Dadun-Khan, a cult. tree.
Hushiarpur, indigenous shrub tree in jungle, called "Kaith."

234. Ægle Marmelos, *Correa.*
T. T. Forest tree, extending to the plains, Moradabad; Simla.
A. Hushiarpur, a common forest tree, not uncommonly cultivated in gardens; Googerat, cult.
Native name "Bael," "Beel." *A.* Not at Jhelum, *J. L. S.*, not at Peshaur.

235. Citrus Aurantium, *L.*
A. A loose-skinned variety of the Orange is largely cultivated throughout the Punjab; called "Naringee." Grown in greater quantity than the last, is a bitter orange, resembling in form and colour the Seville orange, but not nearly so bitter, "Kuttah-Nimboo;" this is largely sold in all the markets along with the Sweet Lime, "Meeta-Nimboo." The true Lime, "Kaguzee-Nimboo," is not quite so common as the above, and more used by Europeans than natives. The Citron and Shaddock are not common at all in the Punjab, the Citron, perhaps, more so than the Shaddock; about Delhi the latter is common enough: called "Pumelo" (Anglo-Indian).
The true Lemon is not known, except to European gardeners. In the Hushiarpur ranges of hills a Citron-like Lemon is largely grown round the dwellings of the natives, producing immense crops of fruit, called "Gulgul;" and this may be one of Royle's forms "met with in the valleys of the Himalaya and tracts of forests," apparently "wild." At Umritsur the "Gulgul" has a great market.
At Googerat the Maltese firm-skinned Orange has been for years cultivated; but to me it seems to have deteriorated from the original stock, tending more to the sweet Lime.

236. Peganum Harmala, *L.*
Royle. The seeds, "Lahoree-Hurmool." Dry districts from Agra to the Ravee.
Edgew. Sangrur; Multan.
T. T. From Agra to the north of the Punjab; Lahore; Jalinder.

A. Jhelum ; Hushiarpur, not very common.
J. L. S. Peshaur.
Vicary. West of Delhi, Sindh.
Fleming. Salt range.
Stocks. Sindh.
Griffith. Afghan.

237. Haplophyllum, species.
J. L. S. Peshaur.

238. H. tuberculatum, *Juss.*
Vicary. Boogta Hills.
Stocks. Beluch. to Kurrachee.

239. Zanthoxylum alatum, *Roxb.*
T. T. Jamu ; Rampur.
St. & Wint. 4000–7000 ft., Kumaon.

SIMARUBEÆ.

240. Ailanthus excelsa, *Roxb.*
Royle. Delhi ; Jumna.
Edgew. Mossewal, near Multan ; wild, Behar.

241. Balanites ægyptiaca, *Delil.*
Ximenia ægyptica, *Roxb.*
X. arborea, *Royle.*
Royle. Delhi.
T. T. Jungle, Thanesar.

242. B. Roxburghii, *Planch.*
Ximenia rigida, *Royle.*
Royle. Delhi.

BURSERACEÆ.

243. Balsamodendron pubescens, *Stocks.*
Stocks. Sindh ; Kurrachee ; Beluchistan.

244. B. Roxburghii, *Stocks.*
Stocks. Indus basin ; Sindh ; Kurrachee ; Tattah.

MELIACEÆ.

245. Cedrela Toona, *Roxb.*
T. T. Jamu ; Kumaon ; Moradabad, cult.
A. Jhelum, Hushiarpur, and Punjab, always cultivated in the plains. "Toon."

246. **Melia Azadirachta**, *L.*
Azadirachta indica, *Juss.*
Edgew. Seikh States, rare (cult.?); Multan, cult.
T. T. Morabadad.
A. Jhelum, one or two known trees (bushes) only, cult.; Philor, Loodiana, and Hushiarpur more common, and as large a tree as *M. Azedarach*; does not seem to ripen its fruit above Philor. It exists as known trees in all large town gardens throughout the Punjab, Lahore, Umritsur, &c. Called " Neem," and is recognized as a southern tree.

247. **M. Azedarach**, *L.*
Edgew. Amballa.
T. T. Jamu, wild; Moradabad, Lahore, cult.
A. Jhelum, Hushiarpur, and throughout the Punjab a most common cultivated tree. In the Hushiarpur hills certainly indigenous.
J. L. S. Peshaur.
Stocks. Beluchistan.
Griff. Afghan.
Throughout the Punjab called "Buchyan," "Dek," by Europeans " Persian Lilac." It loses its leaves completely in winter; and the berries, if not removed, hang in clusters on the tree throughout the winter. Goats, birds, and a large bat are very fond of them. The tree does not flower until its third or fourth year.

248. **M. composita**, *Willd.*
M. superba, *Roxb.*
Edgew. Amballa and Multan, cult.

OLACINEÆ.

249. **Olax nana**, *Wall.*
Edgew. Khizerabad.
T. T. Hurdwar.
A. Hushiarpur, not got so far west before. (I think I got the same plant near Mt. Tilla.)

250. **O. scandens**, *Roxb.*
Jacqt. Delhi to Calcutta, No. 980.

CELASTRACEÆ.

251. **Celastrus paniculatus**, *Willd.*
C. nutans, *Roxb.*
T. T. Moradabad, rare; near the hills, frequent.
Jacq. No. 805.
Vicary. No. 11.
A. Hushiarpur, a characteristic shrub of lower ranges of hills, called " Sinkeeray."

252. C. SENEGALENSIS, *Lam.*
C. montana, *Roxb.*
Caltha montana, *Don.*
Gymnosporia montana, *W. & A.*
Vicary. Delhi, Ferozepur.
Stocks. Sindh.
Griff. Afghan.
Wight. Peninsula.

253. C. SPINOSA, *Royle.*
Gymnosporia spinosa, *H. fil.*
Edgew. Manuswal, Hushiarpur district.
T. T. Chenab valley; Jamu.
A. Jhelum; Hushiarpur, "Pahn."
Fleming. Salt range.
Vicary. Peshaur.
J. L. S. Peshaur.
Griff. Afghan.

254. ELÆODENDRON ROXBURGHII, *W. & A.*
A. Hushiarpur, only on the Purwain range, called "Mir-goo;" Bundelkund, called "Mamri," *Edgew.*

RHAMNEÆ.

255. GOUANIA LANCEOLATA, *Wall.*
Helinus lanceolatus, *H. fil.*
Royle. Delhi.
T. T. Loodiana; Lahore; Jamu.
A. Hushiarpur, on the face of precipitous rocks.
St. & Wint. Kumaon, 1000–4000 ft.
Vicary. Amballa.

256. SAGERETIA BRANDRETHIANA, *Aitch.*
Fleming. Salt range.
A. Jhelum.
J. L. S. Peshaur, "Numani."
Griffith. Afghan, "Maimunna."
Fleming & A. "Kohare." Has an eatable fruit.

257. S. OPPOSITIFOLIA, *Bunge.*
T. T. Simla; Kumaon.
St. & Wint. Kumaon.
J. L. S. Peshaur.

258. S., sp. (no. 6, Hook. list).
T. T. Jamu.
Fleming. Taba; Salt range.
Stocks. Beluchistan.

259. **Rhamnus persica**, *Boiss.*
A. Jhelum.
Stocks. Beluchistan.

260. **R. virgata**, *Roxb.*
T. T. Jamu.
Jacq. No. 2359.
J. L. S. Peshaur.
Vicary. Peshaur Hills.

261. **Zizyphus Jujuba**, *Lam.*
Edgew. Seikh Protected States; Punjab.
T. T. Jamu.
A. Jhelum; Hushiarpur.
J. L. S. Peshaur.
Griffith. Afghan.
Stocks. Indus basin.

Var. **hortensis**, *Edgew.*
Edgew. Multan.
T. T. Lahore.
A. Jhelum, rare; near Russool common. Hushiarpur, Lahore, Loodiana, Umritsur, Philor, in groves like orchards: grown for the fruit, called "Baer;" raised by grafts always. The tree has a very umbrella-like form, and gives a good shade.

Var. **hysudraiacus**, *Edgew.*
Edgew. Multan.
The wild and cultivated fruit both eaten, and sold in all bazars.

262. **Z. Lotus**, *Lam.*
Edgew. Sutlej and west of it, a large tree.

263. **Z. nummularia**, *W. & A.*
Edgew. Multan; Mallawal, rare in the Bar.
T. T. Lahore, profuse; Chenab valley, 3000 feet.
A. Jhelum; Hushiarpur.
Native name, Hushiarpur, "Mulla" and "Jur-Baeree."

264. **Z. Œnoplia**, *Mill.*
Z. Napeca, *Roxb.*
Royle. Delhi.
T. T. Moradabad, common; not at Lahore; Simla.

265. **Zizyphus** (no. 13, *H. list*).
Fruit very large and woody.
T. T. Lahore, jungles.

266. **Z. Spina-Christi**, *Lam.*
Edgew. Multan; Kunnera.
T. T. Cult. Lahore.

267. Z. VULGARIS, *Lam.*
Edgew. Multan, in gardens; Dewal; Khoolduna.
A. Jhelum, Salt range, indigenous.
Fleming. Salt range, *Hb. Edgew.*
J. L. S. Peshaur.
Stocks. Beluch. cultivated.

AMPELIDEÆ.

268. VITIS CARNOSA, *W. & A.*
Edgew. Multan.
T. T. Moradabad; Lahore.
A. Jhelum; Hushiarpur.

269. V. LANATA, *Roxb.*
T. T. Jamu, 2000 to 3000 feet, subtropical.

270. V. LATIFOLIA, *Roxb.*
Edgew. Radaur; Pinjor-Dhun.
T. T. Moradabad; Kumaon, 2500 feet.

271. V. VINIFERA, *L.*
Edgew. Multan, cultivated.
T. T. Chenab valley.
A. Jhelum, Salt range, on limestone, apparently indigenous. Cultivated all over the Punjab. Grapes called "Ungoor."
J. L. S. Peshaur.

272. LEEA, species.
No. 6. *H.f. & T. list.*
T. T. Kumaon; Dehra-Dhun.
Jacq. Rajaori.

SAPINDACEÆ.

273. CARDIOSPERMUM HALICACABUM, *L.*
Edgew. Multan.
T. T. Rampur; Jamu; Lahore.
Falconer. Above Attock.
A. Jhelum; Hushiarpur.
Stocks. Sindh.

274. SAPINDUS ACUMINATA, *Wall.*
T. T. Kumaon.
St. & Wint. Kumaon, 3200 ft.

275. DODONÆA BURMANNIANA, *DC.*
Edgew. Hb. From Peshaur, No. 299.
T. T. Jamu, foot of the hills.

Jacq. Punjab.
A. Jhelum; Umritsur; Hushiarpur; Rūpur.
Griffith. Rūpur.
Fleming. Salt range.
Stocks. Sindh.
J. L. S. Peshaur.
Griffith. Afghan.
A. Amongst the Sewaliks at Bŭdlee and Kŭdlee east of Rūpur. This is its most north-east range, extending westward upon sandstone to Jamu, Jhelum, Attock, Peshaur and Afghanistan.

ANACARDIACEÆ.

276. ODINA WODIER, *Roxb.*
T. T. Jamu.
St. & W. Kumaon, 1000 ft.
A. Hushiarpur: native name "Kembul" and "Kaimul."

277. RHUS INTEGERRIMA, *Wall.*
T. T. Kumaon.
St. & Wint. Kumaon, 5500 ft.
A. Jhelum Hills and Salt range.
J. L. S. (This and not *R. acuminata*) Peshaur; "only a few trees beyond the Indus."

278. R. MYSORENSIS, *Heyne.*
Royle. Delhi.
Stocks. Sindh.

279. PISTACIA KINJUK, *Stocks.*
Stocks's list, No. 719. Indus basin.

280. SPONDIAS MANGIFERA, *Pers.*
Royle. Dehra and Kyarda Dhuns.
A. Hushiarpur: no specimen in herb., but certainly seen in low hill-jungles. Is in Umritsur Government garden; a very large walnut-like tree: native name "Amra."

281. MANGIFERA INDICA, *L.*
Edgew. Multan; fruit very fine.
A. Cult. throughout the Punjab, but usually the fruit poor, as at Jhelum; at Pind-Dadun-Khan fruit very good, so also at Hushiarpur, where clumps of trees exist quite approaching "Topes," with splendid timber.

At the period of ripening, an excess of moisture in the atmosphere seems to be necessary for the perfection of the fruit; at least in loca-

lities where this excess exists in the Punjab the finest fruit is grown, as at Multan, on the canals, Pind-Dadun-Khan, and Hushiarpur.
"Am," Anglo-Indian "Mango."

282. **Buchanania latifolia**, *Roxb.*
Edgew. Khizerabad, "Chiruli."
St. & Wint. Kumaon, 1500 feet.
T. T. Hurdwar.
Jacq. No. 1462 (559).

CORIARIEÆ.

283. **Coriaria nepalensis**, *Wall.*
T. T. Kumaon; Jamu Hills.
St. & W. Kumaon, 3500 feet.
Jacq. Dehra-Dhun.

MORINGEÆ.

284. **Moringa concanensis**, *Nimmo.*
Fleming. Salt range?
Stocks. No. 584.

285. **M. pterygosperma**, *Gaert.*
Edgew. Amballa; Multan, cult.
T. T. Moradabad; Kumaon; Ferozepur, cult.
St. & W. Kumaon, at 1000 ft.
A. Jhelum Hills, Salt range, and Hushiarpur—both indigenous and cultivated. Is a common forest-tree at Hushiarpur, but is cult. in the plains; called "Sohounja."
J. L. S. Peshaur, cultivated.
Stocks. Beluch. to Kurrachee, under 4000 feet.

CALYCIFLORÆ.

LEGUMINOSÆ.

286. **Lotononis Leobordea**, *Benth.*
Stocks. Beluchistan; Sindh.

287. **Heylandia latebrosa**, *DC.*
T. T. Moradabad.
Stocks. Sindh.
Royle. North-west India.

288. **CROTALARIA ALATA**, *Roxb.*
Royle. Kumaon.
T. T. Kumaon.
Edgew. Paota; Alaknanda valley.
A. Hushiarpur, called "Chilchee," no doubt from the noise the dry pods make. Far west and north for this plant.

289. C. **BURHIA**, *Ham.*
Royle. Delhi.
Hamilton. Superior Gangetic plain.
Edgew. Multan; Balanwali.
T. T. Lahore; Ferozepur; Rampur.
Jacq. Punjab.
A. Jhelum.
J. L. S. Not at Peshaur; east of Attock.
Vicary. Bhawulpur.
Stocks. Sindh; Kurrachee.
Griffith. Afghan.

290. C. **HIRSUTA**, *Willd.*
T. T. Kalka.
Edgew. Simla.
Royle. Simla.

291. C. **INCANA**, *L.*
Edgew. Punjab plains.

292. C. **JUNCEA**, *Linn.*
Edgew. Seikh Protected States; Amballa, "Sani."
T. T. Moradabad; Seharanpur; Lahore.
Jacq. Rajaori.
A. Jhelum; Hushiarpur; cultivated throughout the Punjab, but most extensively in the Hushiarpur and Kangra districts, "Sunni."
Stocks. Sindh, a variety with smaller flowers and fruit.
Griffith. Afghan.

293. C. **LUXURIANS**, *Benth.*
Edgew. Punjab, frequent.
T. T. Punjab; Lahore; Moradabad.

294. C. **MEDICAGINEA**, *Lam.*
C. neglecta, *W. & A. Prod.*
T. T. Punjab; Sutlej valley; Rampur.
A. Jhelum; Hushiarpur.
J. L. S. Peshaur.
Edgew. Sirhind.

295. C. **MYSORENSIS**, *Roth.*
Edgew. Loodiana.
T. T. Moradabad; Simla; Sutlej valley; Rampur; Bari Doab.

296. C. PROSTRATA, *Roxb.*
Edgew. Kumaon; Sadhaura.
T. T. Moradabad; plains below Jamu; Chenab.
A. Hushiarpur.

297. C. SERICEA, *Retz.*
T. T. Jamu; Moradabad.
Jacq. Rajaori.
A. Jhelum, cultiv. and wild; Umritsur, wild: flowers in December.

298. C. SESSILIFLORA, *L.*
T. T. Banks of Chenab; Upper Punjab near the hills.

299. ARGYROLOBIUM ROSEUM, *Jb. et Sp.*
Edgew. Nurpur; Zilla Kangra.
T. T. Jamu.
Jacq. Punjab.
Fleming. Salt range; Jelallpur.
A. Jhelum.
Vicary. Boogta Hills.
Stocks. Sindh; Beluchistan.

300. A. ARABICUM, *Jb. et Sp.*
Fleming. Salt range.
A. (*uniflorum,* Jb. et Sp.) Jhelum.
J. L. S. Trans-Indus plains.
Griff. Afghan.

301. TRIGONELLA CORNICULATA, *L.*
Edgew. North-west India; Amballa, from Kashmir seed.

302. T. FŒNUM-GRÆCUM, *L.*
Edgew. Multan; Seikh Protected States, cultiv.; Amballa.
T. T. Lahore; Delhi; Loodiana; Moradabad, also cultivated.
Jacq. (Punjab?) Cult.
J. L. S. Peshaur, cult.
Edgew. Seikh States, "Methi."

303. T. INCISA, *Royle.*
Edgew. Multan; Amballa.
T. T. Ferozepur; Loodiana; Lahore.
Jacq. Cult. Punjab.
A. Jhelum; Hushiarpur.
Griff. Afghan.

304. T. OCCULTA, *Delil.*
Stocks. Sindh.

305. MEDICAGO DENTICULATA, *Willd.*
Edgew. Lahore.

T. T. Lahore; Chenab; Moradabad; pods without spines, Ferozepur.
Jacq. Cult. Punjab.
A. Jhelum.
J. L. S. Peshaur.
A. This plant has extended its area, in and about Umritsur, wherever canal-water has been introduced. It becomes a most noxious weed. When the pods are nearly ripe the fodder is injurious to cattle. It is one of the earliest spring plants, and presents an exquisite green, like that of rice, in its early stage of growth.

306. M. LACINIATA, *All.*
Jacq. Punjab.
Fleming. Salt range.
Stocks. Beluchistan; Sindh.

307. M. LUPULINA, *L.*
Edgew. Multan; Loodiana; banks of the Sha-Nahr; Buhria.
T. T. Moradabad; Ferozepur.
J. L. S. Peshaur.
Griff. Afghan.

308. M. MACULATA, *Willd.*
J. L. S. "Common at Peshaur and Trans Indus; not found before in the plains of India."

309. M. MINIMA, *Willd.*
Jacq. Punjab.
Griff. Afghan.

310. MELILOTUS ALBA, *Lam.*
M. leucantha, *Koch.*
Edgew. Multan.
T. T. Moradabad; Lahore; Loodiana; Meerut.

311. M. PARVIFLORA, *Desf.*
Edgew. Multan.
T. T. Moradabad; Sirhind; Ferozepur; Lahore.
Jacq. No. 1624.
Griff. Afghan.
A. Jhelum.
J. L. S. Peshaur.

312. TRIFOLIUM REPENS, *L.*
J. L. S. "Peshaur and Trans Indus, occasional."

313. LOTUS CORNICULATUS, *L.*
Edgew. Punjab; Multan; Loodiana; Dhurm-Kote.
Vicary. Peshaur.
Stocks. Sindh.
J. L. S. (*angustissimus*, L.?) Peshaur.

314. **L. Garcini,** ***DC.***
L. nubicus, ***Hochst.***
Dalzell. **Sindh.**
Vicary. **Sindh.**
Stocks. **Sindh.**

315. **Psoralea corylifolia,** ***L.***
Edgew. **Punjab; Khujnaur.**
T. T. **Punjab.**
A. **Jhelum.**

316. **P. plicata,** ***Delil.***
Edgew. **Multan.**
T. T. **Lahore; Loodiana.**

317. **Cyamopsis psoraloides,** ***DC.***
Edgew. **Cult. Multan.**
T. T. **Lahore; hort. Moradabad.**
A. **Jhelum (is it indigenous?).**
Griff. **Afghan.**

318. **Indigofera argentea,** ***L.***
Stocks. **Sindh.**

319. **I. cærulea,** ***Roxb.***
Edgew. **Banda.**
Stocks. **Sindh; Beluchistan.**

320. **I. cordifolia,** ***Heyne.***
Royle. **Delhi.**
Edgew. **Multan.**
T. T. **Chenab banks.**
Vicary. **Ferozepur.**
A. **Jhelum.**
Stocks. **Sindh.**

321. **I. enneaphylla,** ***L.***
Edgew. **Multan.**
T. T. **Moradabad; Meerut; Delhi; Jalinder Doab; Loodiana; Lahore.**

322. **I. Gerardiana,** ***Wall.***
T. T. **Everywhere in the North-west Himalaya from 5000 to 9000 ft.; Chini; Rogee.**
J. L. S. **Peshaur.**

323. **I. hirsuta,** ***L.***
T. T. **Moradabad.**
A. **Hushiarpur.**

324. **I. linifolia,** ***Retz.***
Edgew. **Multan.**

T. T. Moradabad ; Ferozepur ; Lahore.
A. Jhelum.
Griff. Afghan.

325. I. PAUCIFOLIA, *Delil.*
Royle. Delhi.
Edgew. Multan ; Morodpur.
Vicary. Sindh.
Stocks. Sindh.

326. I. PENTAPHYLLA, *L.*
Edgew. Loodiana.
T. T. Rowlee-Ghat ; Moradabad ; Loodiana ; Jalinder Doab.

327. I. PULCHELLA, *Roxb.*
Edgew. Sub Sewaliks ; Amballa hort.
T. T. (Var.) Hort. Moradabad.
A. Hushiarpur, indigenous.
Fleming. Salt range.

328. I. SEMITRIJUGA, *Forsk.*
Stocks. Sindh.
Griff. Afghan.

329. I. SENEGALENSIS, *DC.*
I. ornithopodioides, *Schump.*
Edgew. Multan ; Sandal-Bar ; Bŭdowal.
T. T. Lahore.
A. Jhelum.

330. I. TINCTORIA, *L.*
Edgew. Multan.
T. T. Lahore.
A. Cultivated throughout the Punjab, but as a rule in very small quantity ; at Hushiarpur in amount sufficient to yield a marketable article. Near Multan, of late years, its cultivation has been greatly on the increase, as also near Sealkote. "Neel," "Indigo."
J. L. S. Peshaur.

331. I. TRIFOLIATA, *L.*
T. T. Punjab ; banks of Chenab.

332. I. TRITA, *L. fil.*
Royle. Delhi.
Edgew. Banda ; Loodiana.
T. T. Rampur.

333. I. VISCOSA, *Lam.*
T. T. Chenab valley ; Lahore.
Vicary. Sindh.
Griff. Afghan.

334. **Tephrosia apollinea**, *DC.*
Stocks. Sindh.

335. **T. purpurea**, *Pers.*, var. **diffusa**, *W. & A.*
Royle. Delhi.
Edgew. Punjab; Multan; Loodiana.
T. T. Punjab; Loodiana; Moradabad.
A. Jhelum; Hushiarpur.
Stocks. Indus basin.
Edgew. Loodiana, "Maha."
A. In an open plain like the parade-ground at Jhelum, where the plant was in abundance, a mirage representing flowing water was apparent when the wind blew in a direction from the observer, and the light was that of a setting sun, no doubt owing to the silvery appearance of the under surface of the leaves.

336. **T. tenuis**, *Wall.*
Macronyx strigosus, *Dalz.*
Edgew. Punjab; Multan; Sandal Bar (not *M. strictus*). "Kanho."
T. T. Punjab.
A. Jhelum.
Stocks. Sindh.

337. **Millettia.**
Otosema macrophylla, *Bth.*
T. T. Jamu; Kumaon.
St. & Wint. 1000 feet, Kumaon.

338. **Sesbania ægyptiaca**, *L.*
Edgew. Multan; Amballa.
T. T. Moradabad, cult.; Seharanpur; Meerut.
A. Jhelum; Umritsur; Hushiarpur.
J. L. S. Peshaur.
A. In many places becoming quite naturalized, is a common garden plant.
Edgew. Wild near Kharak, "Jait."

339. **S. aculeata**, *Pers.*
Edgew. Multan.
T. T. Lahore; Punjab; Moradabad.
A. Jhelum; Hushiarpur.
J. L. S. Peshaur.
Stocks. Indus basin.

340. **Astragalus camporum**, *Benth.* (sp. near *camporum*).
A. No. 89. Jhelum.
J. L. S. Peshaur.
Bellew. Wuzeerstan.
Griff. Afghan. No. 1523, Kew distribution.

341. A. CONTORTUPLICATUS, *L.*
Edgew. Punjab; Multan.
Stocks. Sindh.

342. A. GRAVEOLENS, *Ham.*
Vicary. Peshaur.
Stocks. Beluchistan.
Griff. Afghan.

343. A. HUMIFUSUS, *Jacq.*
Jacq. Jelallpur.
Vicary. Punjab; Attock.
Griff. Afghan.

344. A. PYROTRICHUS, *Boiss.*
Eyre. Attock; Punjab.
Griff. Afghan.

345. A. LEUCOCEPHALUS, *Grah.*
Jacq. Dehra-Dhun.
Vicary. Loodiana; Peshaur.
A. Jhelum.
Fleming. Salt range, *hb. Edgew.*

346. A. LINEARIS, *Edgew.* (*MS.*).
Fleming. Jabba, on limestone; Salt range, No. 39. *Herb. Edgew.* No. 207.
To the specimen in the Hookerian Herb. at Kew, Bunge has attached a note saying this plant is his *A. bakuensis.*

347. A. MULTICEPS, *Wall.*
Jacq. Salt range.
Fleming. Salt range.
A. Jhelum.
Vicary. Jhelum; Peshaur.

348. A. PROLIXUS, *Sieb.*
Edgew. Loodiana; Multan.
T. T. Punjab; Ferozepur.
Stocks. Sindh.

349. A. RAMOSUS, *L.*
T. T. Lahore; Punjab.

350. A. TRIBULOIDES, *Del.*
A. minutus, *Boiss.*
Edgew. Punjab; Multan; banks of Ravi; Dulwan.
T. T. Ferozepur; Loodiana; Lahore.
Jacq. Punjab.
A. Jhelum.
J. L. S. Peshaur.

351. **Taverniera nummularia**, *DC.*
T. glabra, *Boiss.*
Fleming. North of Salt range; Futtypur.
A. Jhelum.
Vicary. Peshaur; Boogta hills.
Stocks. Beluchistan; Sindh.
Jacq. Punjab.

352. **Onobrychis sativa**, *Lam.*
Vicary. Peshaur, cultiv.

353. **Alhagi maurorum**, *Tourn.*
Royle. Delhi.
Edgew. Multan; Amballa.
T. T. Lahore.
A. Jhelum; Hushiarpur.
J. L. S. Peshaur.
Griffith. Punjab. "Joussa;" "prickly leguminous, with the habit of *Fagonia.*"
Stocks. Indus basin.
Royle. Native name, "Juwansa."
Edgew. Amballa, "Joasa."

354. **Æschynomene indica**, *L.*
Edgew. Multan.
T. T. Moradabad; Rampur; Jamu; Kumaon; Lahore.

355. **Zornia diphylla**, *Pers.*
T. T. Jalinder; Dehra-Dhun; Rampur; Moradabad.

356. **Desmodium gangeticum**, *DC.*
Edgew. Amballa; Sadhaura; Kyarda-Dhun.
T. T. Lahore; Moradabad.
Jacq. No. 1586.
A. Hushiarpur.

357. **D. latifolium**, *DC.*
Edgew. Pinjor-Dhun.
T. T. Moradabad.

358. **D. tiliæfolium**, *Don.*
Edgew. Punjab Himalaya.
Fleming. Marri.
A. Hushiarpur, called "Sunun;" the fibre used to make twine and paper. Another *Desmodium* in hb. Edgew. is called by the natives "Sunnun-Bundelee," showing the natives are aware that these plants yield a fibre like that of the "Sun," *Crotalaria juncea.*

359. **D. triflorum**, *DC.*
T. T. Moradabad; Dehra-Dhun; Umballa; Loodiana; Jalinder.

360. **Uraria Lagopus**, *DC.*
Edgew. Simla; Karnal (86).
T. T. Rowlee-Ghat; Jamu; Dehra-Dhun.
Jacq. No. 1589.
A. Hushiarpur.

361. **U. picta**, *Desv.*
Edgew. Radaur, amongst *Butea.*
T. T. Sutlej valley; Rampur; Moradabad.

362. **Alysicarpus bupleurifolius**, *DC.*
A. gracilis, *Edgew.*
Edgew. Banda; Multan.
T. T. Lahore; Moradabad.
J. L. S. Peshaur.

363. **A. monilifer**, *DC.*
Edgew. Banda.
T. T. Meerut; Moradabad.
Jacq. No. 1580.

364. **A. scariosus**, *Grah.*
Edgew. Banda.
Stocks. Sindh; Kurrachee.

365. **A. vaginalis**, *DC.*
A. nummulariæfolius, *DC.*
Edgew. Banda.
T. T. Moradabad; Dehra-Dhun; Rampur; Sirhind; Punjab.
A. Jhelum.

366. **A. Wallichii**, *W. & A.*
T. T. Punjab; Moradabad.

367. **Lespedeza cuneata**, *Don.*
L. juncea, *Pers.*
T. T. Rampur.
Fleming. Marri.
A. Jhelum.
J. L. S. Peshaur.

368. **Cicer arietinum**, L.
Edgew. Seikh Protected States; Multan, cult.
T. T. Lahore; Moradabad.
A. Jhelum; Hushiarpur; throughout the Punjab largely cultivated. "Chŭnna," Auglo-Indian "Gram."
J. L. S. Peshaur, cult.

369. **Vicia Faba, *L.***
T. T. Cult. Nubra; Simla.
J. L. S. Peshaur, cult.
A. The Bean: only cultivated for Europeans.

370. **V. narbonensis, *L.***
Vicary. Peshaur.

371. **V. sativa, *L.***
Edgew. Multan; Sadhaura.
T. T. Moradabad; Lahore; Simla.
A. Jhelum; Hushiarpur.
J. L. S. Peshaur.
Stocks. Sindh.
Griff. Afghan.

372. **Vicia.**
Ervum hirsutum, *L.*
Edgew. Multan; Amballa.
T. T. Lahore.
Wallich. Meerut.
Griff. Afghan.
A. Hushiarpur.

373. **Vicia.**
Ervum Lens, *L.*
Edgew. Multan, cult.
T. T. Lahore; Moradabad; Ferozepur; Simla.
A. Jhelum; Hushiarpur, cult.
J. L. S. Peshaur, cult.
Stocks. Beluchistan.
Griff. Afghan.

374. **Lathyrus annuus?, *L.***
A. Jhelum; Hushiarpur.

375. **L. Aphaca, *L.***
Edgew. Multan; Amballa.
T. T. Lahore; Ferozepur; Moradabad.
Lady Dalhousie. Umballa.
A. Jhelum; Hushiarpur.
Griff. Afghan.

376. **L. sativus, *L.***
Edgew. Multan, cult; Seikh Protected States, a weed, also cult.
T. T. Cult. at Lahore, and also occurring as a weed of cultivation; Moradabad.
A. Hushiarpur Hills, quite a weed, also cultivated.
Griff. Afghan.
Edgew. "Matar" of Bengal.

377. L. SPHÆRICUS, *Retz.*
Edgew. Jagadhri; Mulana; Multan.
T. T. Moradabad.
A. Hushiarpur.

378. LATHYRUS.
Orobus luteus, *L.*
Fleming. Salt range.

379. PISUM SATIVUM, *L.*
P. arvense, *L.*
Royle. Delhi, indigenous; cultivated in the hills.
Edgew. Lahore, corn-fields; Multan, cult.
T. T. Simla.
Stocks. Beluchistan.
Griff. Afghan.
Royle. Delhi, native name "Urra-Muttur," in hills "Kullae."

380. ABRUS PRECATORIUS, *L.*
Edgew. Multan.
T. T. Moradabad.
A. Hushiarpur, plant "Rutthuck," seeds "Ruttee;" common in the jungle.

381. CLITORIA TERNATEA, *L.*
Edgew., A. Cultivated in gardens throughout the Punjab.

382. GLYCINE LABIALIS, *Roxb.*
G. mollis, *W. & A.*
Edgew. Jagadhri; Amballa.
T. T. Loodiana; Sirhind; Moradabad.

383. ERYTHRINA INDICA, *Lam.*
Edgew. Multan, cult.

384. E. SUBEROSA, *Roxb.*
T. T. Kumaon; Moradabad.
St. & Wint. Kumaon, 2500 feet.
A. Hushiarpur Hills, indigenous, "Noosus;" cultivated throughout the Punjab.

385. MUCUNA PRURIENS, *Wall.*
Edgew. Sadhaura.
T. T. Jamu; Rampur.
Jacq. Rajaori.
A. Jhelum; Mt. Tilla; Hushiarpur, "Googlee," "Kooglee," profuse.

386. **Butea frondosa**, *Roxb.*
Edgew. Seikh Protected States; Loodiana; Multan.
T. T. Jalinder.
Jacq. Punjab.
A. Jhelum; Hushiarpur.
Griff. "Bukrala-Khud," near Jhelum; is the "Chuchra" of the natives and used for paper.
J. L. S. Peshaur, very rare.
A. Hushiarpur, "Chichera."

387. **Canavalia gladiata**, *DC.*
Edgew. Multan, cult.
T. T. Hort. Moradabad; Kalingar, apparently wild; Soane, frequent.

388. **Phaseolus aconitifolius**, *Jacq.*
Edgew. Seikh Protected States; Multan, cultivated.
T. T. Moradabad, cult.
A. Jhelum; Hushiarpur, cult.
J. L. S. Peshaur, cult.
Edgew. Seikh States, "Moth."

389. **P. Mungo**, *L.*
P. radiatus, *L.*
P. Roxburghii, *W. & A.*
Edgew. Seikh Protected States, cult.; Loodiana; Amballa, cult.; Multan, cult.
T. T. Cult., Rechnab Doab; Lahore; Kalka; Moradabad.
A. Jhelum; Hushiarpur, cult.
J. L. S. Peshaur.
Edgew. Seikh States, "Urud."
A. Jhelum, "Múng."

390. **P. trilobus**, *Ait.*
Edgew. Khundote; Banda.
A. Jhelum; Mt. Tilla, at its base, indigenous.
Stocks. Sindh, cult. (likely *P. aconitifolius*, Jacq.).

391. **Vigna carinalis**, *Benth.*
V. angustifolia, *Wall.*
Lady Dalhousie. Simla.
T. T. Rampur; Simla.
A. Jhelum.

392. **V. sinensis**, *Benth.*
V. Catjang, *Benth.*
Edgew. Amballa; Seikh Protected States.
T. T. Lahore; Kalka; Moradabad.

393. **Dolichos biflorus**, *L.*
D. uniflorus, *Lam.*
Edgew. Seikh States, cult., called "Kulte."
Lady Dalhousie. Ganges.
T. T. Kalka.
A. Jhelum.

394. **D. Lablab**, *L.*
Lablab vulgaris, *Savi.*
Edgew. Jagadhri; Bilaspur; Seikh Protected States; Multan, cult.
T. T. Moradabad.
Jacq. No. 1377 (where?).
J. L. S. Peshaur (a species, perhaps this), cult.

395. **Cajanus indicus**, *Spr.*
C. flavus, *D.C.*
C. bicolor, *Wall.*
T. T. Moradabad; Punjab.
Edgew. Seikh Protected States, cult., called "Tuar," Anglo-Indian "Horse-grain"; cult. on hills, called "Kui."
A. Hushiarpur, in low hills, quite a weed of cultivation, called "Dinger," also cultivated.
J. L. S. Peshaur, cult.

396. **Atylosia scarabæoides**, *Benth.*
T. T. Jamu; Deyrah-Dhun; Moradabad.

397. **Rhynchosia.**
Nomismia aurea, *W. & A.*
A. Jhelum, curiously buries its seed whilst ripening, if trailing against the ground.

398. **Rhynchosia.**
R. minima, *DC.*
R. medicaginea, *Lam.*
R. microphylla, *Heyne.*
R. nuda, *DC.*
Royle. Delhi.
Edgew. Multan.
T. T. Moradabad; Ferozepur; Lahore.
Jacq. No. 1383 (where?).
A. Jhelum; Hushiarpur.
J. L. S. Peshaur.
Stocks. Sindh.

400. **Rhynchosia.**
Nomismia nummularia, *W. & A.*
Edgew. Bŭdowal; Loodiana.
T. T. Lahore; Punjab.

401. **R. pulverulenta**, *Stocks.*
Stocks. Sindh.

402. **R. Rothii**, *Benth.*
R. sericea, *Spreng.*
Edgew. Amballa; Multan.
T. T. Lahore; Rampur; Moradabad.
Jacq. Rajaori.
A. Hushiarpur.

403. **Dalbergia Sissoo**, *Roxb.*
Edgew. Seikh Protected States; Multan.
T. T. Moradabad; Meerut; Lahore.
A. Jhelum; Hushiarpur.
J. L. S. Peshaur.
A. Is a largely cultivated tree throughout the Punjab, called "Sheshum," "Sissoo," "Tali." With water at no great depth and good soil, it produces very fine timber (and rapidly, *J. L. S.*); but with an absence of water, and loose stony soil that has difficulty of retaining moisture, as in the Jhelum district generally, it is not worth the trouble of growing. At Hushiarpur and on the Umritsur canals the young trees might be transplanted up to the fourth year, and division of the tap-root did not interfere with the success of the operation; cutting the tap-root at all, or transplanting after two years, the plants never succeeded in the Jhelum district.
It is indigenous to the Punjab, chiefly on the lower hills (to 5000 ft. *Edgew.*); it extends through the Salt range, Raulpindee, Attock, Peshaur to Afghanistan and Beluchistan, and occurs in Sindh. The largest *Sissoo* tree that I have seen measured (4 feet from the ground) is 18 feet in circumference, and is at Kutas in the Salt range. It is within a small building and therefore apt to be overlooked, unless particularly asked for.

404. **Pongamia glabra**, *Vent.*
Jacq. No. 1393 (where?).
A. Hushiarpur, is a cultivated tree, common, and may be indigenous, called "Sook-chyne." The wood is said to be impervious to white ants.

405. **Sophora.**
Edwardsia hydaspica, *Edgew.*
Edgew. Hort. Multan, from Salt range.

406. EDWARDSIA MOLLIS, *Royle*.
Royle. North-west Himalaya.
T. T. Chenab valley.
Fleming. Salt range.
A. Salt range (not *hydaspica*, Edgew.).
J. L. S. Peshaur.
Vicary. Boogta Hills; Rawulpindee.
After a very careful examination of the Kew Herbarium, I cannot distinguish my Salt-range species from *E. mollis*, Royle (Royle's original specimens), and therefore refer them to Royle's *E. mollis*.

407. CÆSALPINIA.
Guilandina Bonducella, *L.*
T. T. Moradabad.
A. Jhelum; Salt range, from cultivation perhaps; Hushiarpur Jungle, indigenous; Loodiana, cult., "Kut-Karounja."

408. CÆSALPINIA SEPIARIA, *Roxb.*
Edgew. Nurpur; Zilla Hushiarpur.
T. T. Chenab valley.
A. Hushiarpur, "Bumool;" Bŭdlee.

409. POINCIANA PULCHERRIMA, *L.*
A. Cultivated, Punjab gardens, common.

410. PARKINSONIA ACULEATA, *L.*
A. Cultivated throughout the Punjab to Peshaur (*J. L. S.*), and is apparently becoming naturalized.

411. CASSIA ABSUS, *L.*
T. T. Rampur; Sairi; Moradabad.
Jacq. No. 1403 (524).

412. C. FISTULA, *L.*
A. Throughout the plains of the Punjab cultivated as an ornamental tree, called "Indian Laburnum," "Amultas."
Edgew. Multan.
In the low hills of Hushiarpur, and to Jamu (*T. T.*) indigenous.
It does not extend to Peshaur (*J. L. S.*); nor did I find it on the hills near Jhelum or Salt range.

413. C. LANCEOLATA, *Forsk.*, *Royle*.
C. acutifolia, *Delile*.
C. elongata, *Lam.*
A. Jhelum, cultivated.
Stocks. Sindh.
Narrow-leaved "Senna."

414. C. MIMOSOIDES, *L.*
T. T. Dehra-Dhun; Kotghur; Rampur.
St. & Wint. Kumaon.
A. Jhelum; Mt. Tilla.

415. C. OBTUSA, *Roxb.*
C. obovata, *Coll.*
Fleming. Salt range.
Vicary. Sindh.
Stocks. Sindh.
Broad-leaved "Senna."

416. C. OCCIDENTALIS, *L.*
C. sophora, *L.*
T. T. Lahore.
Edgew. Multan.
Stocks. Indus basin.

417. C. PUBESCENS, *R. Br.*
Stocks. Sindh.

418. C. PUMILA, *Lam.*
T. T. Moradabad; Lahore.

419. C. SUFFRUTICOSA, *Koen.*
Edgew. Nahn, wild; Multan, cult.
T. T. Hort. Moradabad.
Wall. Dehra-Dhun.
Jacq. No. 1405 (2504).

420. C. TORA, *L.*
Edgew. Multan.
T. T. Moradabad; Meerut; Loodiana; Lahore.
A. Jhelum; Hushiarpur, called "Along."
Stocks. Indus basin.

421. CERATONIA SILIQUA, *L.*
A. Of late years the "Carob" has been largely introduced into the Punjab. There are (or were) a few trees at Lahore old enough to bear fruit, which they have done; these must have been introduced with *Albizzia procera,* Benth., or about that period.

422. BAUHINIA PURPUREA, *L.*
Edgew. Sadhaura.
T. T. Hurdwar, cult.
A. A cultivated tree throughout the Punjab, not uncommon in gardens. The flower-buds are eaten by the natives cooked, called "Kochnar."

423. B. RACEMOSA, *Lam.*
B. parviflora, *Vahl.*
Edgew. Kumaon.
A. Hushiarpur low hills, common, "Kosūndra." A small tree, not a climber.

424. B. VAHLII, *W. & A.*
B. racemosa, *Vahl.*
Edgew. Sewaliks.
T. T. Kumaon.
St. & Wint. Kumaon, at 2500 feet.
A. Hushiarpur Forest and in the hill jungle, common, an immense climber, called "Thour." The bark used for ropes, and the leaves for wrapping up parcels of small goods, instead of paper, in the bazars, covering umbrellas, &c. &c.

425. B. VARIEGATA, *L.*
Edgew. Multan; Amballa.
A. Jhelum; Hushiarpur. Cultivated throughout the Punjab gardens. Its flowers used in the same way as those of *B. purpurea*, perhaps a more common tree, also called "Kochnar."
J. L. S. Peshaur.

426. TAMARINDUS INDICA, *L.*
A. A cultivated tree, not common in the Punjab, met with at Pind-Dadan-Khan. This is most likely its northern range. Multan (*Edgew.*), Hushiarpur (*A.*), "Tamarind," "Imlee."
Stocks. Beluchistan to Kurrachee.

427. PROSOPIS SPICIGERA, *L.*
Royle. Delhi.
Edgew. Seikh Protected States; Amballa; Multan.
T. T. Ferozepur; Punjab; Lahore.
A. Jhelum; Googerat; Sindh. "Kunda," fruit "Singhar."
Stocks. Sindh.
A. Jhelum, "Jand," *Edgew.*; Seikh States, "Jhand."
Griffith. Lahore, "Jundy?" (perhaps this plant).

428. P. STEPHANIANA, *Bth.*
J. L. S. Peshaur.
Griffith. Afghan.

429. DICHROSTACHYS CINEREA, *W. & A.*
Royle. Delhi.
Edgew. Futtehghur.
Stocks. Indus basin.

430. MIMOSA RUBICAULIS, *Lam.*
T. T. Punjab.

Jacq. Subatoo.
Fleming. Salt range.
A. Mt. Tilla; Hushiarpur; Goodaspore.
Stocks. Sindh.
Griffith. Afghan.
A. Hushiarpur, "Durguree."

431. ACACIA ARABICA, *L*.
A. Throughout the Punjab (*Edgew*., *T. T.*) an indigenous and most extensively cultivated tree; does not seem to extend to Peshaur (*J. L. S.*). On Tilla, Jhelum, not above 1200 feet.
The variety *cupressina* extends from Rupur (*A*.), its eastern limit, to (*Stocks, A.*) Sindh, and apparently is known in the north, as it is called by the Sindhians "Kablee-Bubbur."
The common *Acacia arabica* is called "Babool," Hind.; "Keekur," Punjabee; "Bubbur," Sindhian.

432. A. CÆSIA, *W. & A.*
Edgew. Himalaya, 3000 feet; Banasar.
T. T. Jamu.
A. Hushiarpur, "Durgaree," common in hills.

433. A. CATECHU, *Willd*.
C. catechuoides, *Roxb*.
Edgew. Pinjor-Dhun, "Khyr."
Royle. Northern India, "Khuer;" Delhi.
T. T. Jamu; Punjab.
A. Hushiarpur, common, "Khier."
Fleming. Salt range.
J. L. S. Peshaur, rare.

434. A. EBURNEA, *Willd*.
T. T. Hurdwar.
A. Jhelum; Salt range.
Griffith. Afghan.

435. A. FARNESIANA, *Willd*.
Edgew. Wild, Fureed-kote, Multan, and Kangra hills; Multan cult.
T. T. Moradabad and Punjab, cult.
Jacq. No. 1415 (137").
A. Punjab cult.; common in gardens and near dwellings, Jhelum, Hushiarpur, Umritsur, Philor; low hills, Hushiarpur district, appeared indigenous.
Stocks. Sindh.

436. A. JACQUEMONTII, *Decais*.
Edgew. Multan; Jhung.

T. T. Punjab.
Jacq. Rajaori.
J. L. S. Peshaur.

437. A. LEUCOPHLŒA, *Willd.*
Royle. Delhi.
Edgew. Seikh Protected States; Pinjor-Dhun; Loodiana.
T. T. Moradabad; Punjab; Jamu.
Jacq. Poonch; Delhi.
A. Umritsur; Philor; Loodiana; Hushiarpur; Kalka.
Edgew. Seikh Protected States, called "Rerul."
A. Hushiarpur, "Areer," "Kareer."

438. A. MODESTA, *Wall.*
Royle. Delhi.
Edgew. Seikh Protected States; Multan.
T. T. Jamu; Lahore; Loodiana.
Vicary. Amballa.
A. Jhelum; Hushiarpur; Umritsur; Philor.
J. L. S. Peshaur.
Edgew. Seikh States, "Phalahi."

439. A. RUPESTRIS, *Stocks.*
Stocks. Beluch. to Kurrachee, under 4000 ft., *Hb. Stocks,* No. 502.

440. ALBIZZIA LEBBEK, *Benth.*
A. serissa, *Roxb.*
Edgew. Multan; Amballa.
T. T. Punjab.
J. L. S. Peshaur, cult.
A. Cultivated extensively throughout the Punjab, called "Seriss," a fine, shady, and, in some localities, lofty tree, but generally not lofty, and spreading.
Indigenous in low ranges of hills, Hushiarpur, *A.*; Jamu, *T. T.*; Jhelum district, Mt. Tilla, *J. L. S.*

441. A. PROCERA, *Benth.*
Acacia elata, *Grah.*
Royle. Dehra-Dhun.
Edgew. Dehra-Dhun.
A. A tree introduced into the Punjab chiefly by Mr. Edgeworth; Multan, Googaira, Hushiarpur, &c. &c., at Umritsur, Jalinder, and Amballa. In general appearance, loftiness, and rapidity of growth, with elegance, it far surpasses any Punjab tree. Its wood is said to be quite as valuable, if not more so, than that of the "Seriss."

442. INGA DULCIS, *Willd.*
Royle. Delhi, in gardens, cult.

ROSACEÆ.

443. **Prunus (Amygdalus) communis**, *L.*

A. A common garden plant throughout the Punjab. The fruit called "Bedam."

J. L. S. Peshaur.

Griffith. Afghan.

444. **Prunus.**

Cerasus Mahaleb, *Mill.*

Stocks. Sindh, cult. at Kelat, with scented kernels, called "Mahalib."

445. **P. domestica**, *L.*, var.

A. A species of plum, both a green and red variety, size and shape of a Greengage, is common in the Punjab gardens, bearing very heavy crops of fruit, called "Aloo-Bokara."

Edgew. Amballa.

A. Hushiarpur; Jalinder; Umritsur; Googerat; Jhelum.

446. **Prunus.**

Armeniaca vulgaris, *Lam.*

T. T. Kumaon and Gurwhal to 12,000 ft., cultivated.

A. Salt range; Punjab, cult.; Hushiarpur, cult., otherwise not in the plains of the Punjab, "Zurd-aloo." The English Apricot has been introduced into gardens at Jalinder.

The dried Apricot is called "Khoobanee," a large import article from the north.

447. **Prunus.**

Persica vulgaris, *Mill.*

Amygdalus collinus, *Wall.*

T. T. Cultivated throughout the whole Himalaya, (*A.*) also the Punjab gardens, with frequently the flat China Peach and the Nectarine.

J. L. S. Peshaur, extensive orchards.

The Peach, "Aroo."

The Nectarine, "Moondla-Aroo." Royle gives the same names as being applied to them in the North-west Provinces of India.

448. **Rubus flavus**, *Ham.*

T. T. Kumaon and Jamu Hills.

A. Hushiarpur; Purwain range of hills. Yields the Yellow Bramble of the Himalaya. The fruit is very early in the year, that of the other sp. quite late, "Zurd-anchoo," *Royle.*

449. **R. fruticosus**, *L.*

T. T. Jamu Hills, 4000 ft.; Kashmir.

J. L. S. Peshaur.
Griff. Afghan.
The Bramble, Blackberry.

450. R. LASIOCARPUS, *Sm.*
J. L. S. Peshaur, perhaps the seeds brought down the stream from a higher locality.

451. R. NIVEUS, *Wall.*
Fleming. Marri Hills.
A. Jhelum; Fort Mungla. The seeds brought down from a higher locality by the river and germinated on the banks.
T. T. Fruit eatable and good, claret-coloured when ripe.

452. POTENTILLA SUPINA, *L.*
Edgew. Multan; Thanesar; Nahn.
T. T. Moradabad; Jamu plains; Lahore.
Vicary. Punjab.
A. Jhelum; Hushiarpur.
J. L. S. Peshaur.
Stocks. Sindh.
Griff. Afghan.

453. FRAGARIA VESCA, *L.*
A. The Strawberry, cultivated by Europeans only; produces very fair fruit in the Punjab.

454. ROSA, species.
A. The Rose, "Goolab," is cultivated throughout the Punjab for the distillation of rose-water; *Edgew. R. indica*, L., and *damascena*, Mill., cult. Multan; *H.f. & T.*, in Hooker's list of Indian Plants, give as cult. in India *R. indica*, L., *multiflora*, L., *microphylla*, Roxb., and *centifolia*, L.
Royle gives *R. damascena*, Mill., as cultivated in the North-west Provinces.

455. NEURADA PROCUMBENS, *L.*
Edgew. Multan; Adunwhan Hills.
Vicary. Sindh.
Stocks. Sindh; Beluch.

456. PYRUS COMMUNIS, *L.*
T. T. Kashmir, cult.
A. Hushiarpur, and occasionally in gardens in the Punjab. Fruit large but very woody. "Nashpatee," so called from the name applied to the Pears imported from Kăbul and that direction.

457. P. **Malus**, *L.*
T. T. Kashmir, cult.
Griff. Afghan.
Edgew. Multan, cult.
A. A small apple is cultivated throughout the Punjab, and plains of North-west India, in gardens, called "Sayoo" or "Seb."

458. **Pyrus.**
Cydonia vulgaris, *Pers.*
Edgew. Hort. Amballa.
T. T. Kashmir, cult.
A. The Quince is frequently met with cultivated in Punjab gardens; the fruit, however, is poor, called "Bheehee."

459. **Photinia.**
Eriobotrya japonica, *Lind.*
Edgew. Cult. at Amballa.
A. Cult., grafted at Jhelum; Googerat and Hushiarpur on its own stock. There are two varieties of the fruit, "Loquat"—one small and nearly round, the other larger and pear-shaped.

SAXIFRAGACEÆ.

460. **Vahlia viscosa**, *Roxb.*
V. Weldenii, *Reich.*
T. T. Amballa; Punjab.
Vicary. Amballa; Sindh.
Edgew. Banda.

CRASSULACEÆ.

461. **Tillæa pentandra**, *Royle.*
Royle. Kumaon.
T. T. Simla.
Vicary. Punjab to Peshaur.

462. T. **pharnaceoides**, *Hochst.*
Edgew. North-west Himalaya.
A. Hushiarpur.
Vicary. Peshaur.
J. L. S. mentions a *Tillæa* at Peshaur; it may be this or the last.

463. **Sedum pallidum**, *Bieb.*
Vicary. Punjab near Peshaur.

464. S. **multicaule**, *Wall.*
T. T. Kumaon; Simla, 5000 to 7000 feet.
Vicary. Peshaur.

HALORAGEÆ.

465. **Myriophyllum tuberculatum**, *Wall.*
T. T. Banks of Chenab.
Stocks. Beluchistan.
Griff. Afghan.

RHIZOPHOREÆ.

466. **Rhizophora mucronata**, *Lam.*
T. T. Ganges; Sunderbunds.
Stocks. Delta of Indus.

467. **Ceriops Candolliana**, *Arn.*
Stocks. Sindh.
Vicary. Sindh.

468. **Bruguiera Rheedei**, *Blum.*
T. T. Ganges; Sunderbunds.
Stocks. Delta, Indus river.

COMBRETACEÆ.

469. **Terminalia Bellerica**, *Roxb.*
Edgew. Amballa (cult.?), " Bahera."
T. T. Kumaon.
Falc. Garwhal.
A. Hushiarpur forest, and low hills, indigenous. Frequently cultivated in the south-east of the Punjab. Fruit, " Behara," valued for tanning and dyeing.

470. **T. Chebula**, *Retz.*
St. & Wint. Kumaon, 3000 to 5000 feet.
A. Hushiarpur forests, an indigenous tree. The fruit, " Hur," valued for tanning and dyeing.

471. **Terminalia.**
Pentaptera glabra, *W. & A.*
H. f. & T. T. Rajmahal and Monghir.
A. Hushiarpur, a large tree in Purwain forest, indigenous.

472. **Anogeissus acuminata**, *Wall.*
Conocarpus acuminatus, *Roxb.*
Edgew. Banda.
Stocks. Deesa.

473. A. latifolia, *Wall.*
Conocarpus latifolia, *Roxb.*
Edgew. Pinjor-Dhun.
St. & Wint. Kumaon, 1000 feet.

474. A. pendula, *Edgew.*
A. myrtifolia, *Wall.*
Royle. Jumna, may have spread from below.

MYRTACEÆ.

475. Psidium pomiferum, *L.*
T. T. Cultivated as far north as the Indus river.
A. Cultivated generally in all the gardens of the Punjab, getting less frequent towards the north. At and around Delhi the fruit "Amrud," Anglo-Indian "Guava," is of superior quality, and of several varieties.

476. Myrtus communis, *L.*
A. A cultivated shrub throughout the gardens of the Punjab, "Henna."
Stocks. Beluch.
Griff. Afghan.

477. Eugenia.
Syzygium Jambolana, *DC.*
T. T. Kumaon.
St. & Wint. Kumaon, at 1000 feet.
A. A common cultivated tree, meagre and produces no fruit at Jhelum. At Umritsur and Hushiarpur a fine lofty tree yielding large quantities of a deep-purple-coloured fruit, the size of a large damson, and much resembling it in appearance, called "Jaman" and "Golab-Jaman."

LYTHRARIEÆ.

478. Ammannia.
Ameletia indica, *DC.*
T. T. Chenab; Moradabad.

479. Ammannia.
Ameletia rotundifolia, *Wight.*
Edgew. Multan; Radaur.
T. T. Jamu; Moradabad.
A. Hushiarpur.

480. Ammannia.
Rotala Roxburghii, *Wight.*
R. pentandra, *Roxb.*
Edgew. Multan; Ramghur.
T. T. Chenab; Upper Punjab; Moradabad.

481. AMMANNIA.
A. glauca, *Wall.*
Edgew. Banda.
T. T. Jamu; Moradabad.

482. A. MULTIFLORA, *Roxb.*
A. auriculata, *Willd.*
Edgew. Multan.
T. T. Banks of Chenab.
J. L. S. Peshaur.

483. A. VESICATORIA, *Roxb.*
Edgew. Multan; Sadhaura; Mo-barik-pur.
T. T. Lahore; Chenab; Moradabad.
A. Hushiarpur.
J. L. S. Peshaur.
Stocks. Indus basin.

484. WOODFORDIA FLORIBUNDA, *Salisb.*
Grislea tomentosa, *Roxb.*
T. T. Kumaon.
A. Jhelum; Mungla; Hushiarpur.
Fleming. Salt range.
J. L. S. At the *débouchement* of the Swat river.
A. Hushiarpur, "Tawa," "Dhawa," "Dham," "Dhamee:" yields a dye.

485. LAWSONIA ALBA, *Lam.*
L. inermis, *L.*
Royle. Much cultivated to the north of the Jumna.
Edgew. Seikh Protected States, cultivated extensively (see Edgeworth's papers, J. Asiatic Society of Calcutta), called "Mehndi."
T. T. Cultivated everywhere in India.
A. A common garden shrub in the Punjab.
J. L. S. Cult. Peshaur.
Stocks. Beluchistan, indigenous.

486. PUNICA GRANATUM, *L.*
T. T. Kumaon, 5500 feet, indigenous.
St. & Wint. Kumaon.
Edgew. Multan, cult.
A. Jhelum; Mt. Tilla and Salt range, may be indigenous; Hushiarpur, common on hills, but near dwellings. Is a common garden shrub in the Punjab. In some gardens yields a large and good fruit called "Anar." But the mass of Pomegranates used in the country are imported from Kabul and that direction.
Stocks. Beluchistan.
Griff. Afghan.

ONAGRARIEÆ.

487. EPILOBIUM TOMENTOSUM, *Boiss.*
Fleming. Salt range.
T. T. Rampur.
J. L. S. Peshaur.
Griff. Afghan.

488. JUSSIÆA REPENS, *L.*
T. T. Moradabad; Loodiana.
A. Hushiarpur.

489. LUDWIGIA PARVIFLORA, *Roxb.*
Edgew. Dowranee.
T. T. Moradabad.

490. ŒNOTHERA SINUATA, *L.*
A. Hushiarpur, certainly an escape, as it is an American plant. It will be curious if this also fixes itself in India.

491. TRAPA NATANS, *L.*, var. BISPINOSA.
T. T. Kashmir; Moradabad; Lahore.
A. Jhelum, seeds float down the river from the Kashmir lakes, but do not germinate; cultivated frequently in tanks in the Punjab.
J. L. S. Peshaur, perhaps introduced.
A. Hushiarpur, "Singhara."

SAMYDACEÆ.

492. CASEARIA TOMENTOSA, *Roxb.*
Royle. North-west Provinces of India; Dehra-Dhun.
T. T. Jamu; Kumaon.
St. & Wint. Kumaon, at 1000 ft.
A. Jhelum; Hushiarpur.

CUCURBITACEÆ.

493. TRICHOSANTHES CUCUMERINA, *L.*
T. T. Moradabad, indigenous.
A. Hushiarpur, indigenous, "Kundoree."

494. TRICHOSANTHES.
No. 4. *H. f. & T.*, distribution.
T. T. Ferozepur; Moradabad; Loodiana.

495. LAGENARIA VULGARIS, *Sering.*
Edgew. Multan, cult., "Kuddu."
T. T. Moradabad.

496. LUFFA ACUTANGULA, *Sering.*
Edgew. Multan, cult.; Amballa, cult.

497. L. AMARA, *Roxb.*
T. T. Jamu; Punjab.
A. Jhelum.
Stocks. Indus basin.

498. L. ECHINATA, *Roxb.*
Stocks. Deesa; Sindh.

499. L. CYLINDRICA, *Naud.*
L. pentandra, *Roxb.*
Edgew. Multan, cult.
T. T. Moradabad, garden.

500. BENINCASA CERIFERA, *Savi.*
T. T. Punjab, cult., an enormous gourd.

501. MOMORDICA BALSAMINA, *L.*
T. T. Punjab.
Stocks. Sindh, indigenous.

502. M. CHARANTIA, *L.*
T. T. Punjab and Jamu, indigenous. Cultivated everywhere.
Edgew. Multan, indigenous and cult.

503. M. DIOICA, *Roxb.*
Edgew. Radaur.
T. T. Moradabad; Punjab; Lahore.
A. Jhelum; Hushiarpur.

504. CUCUMIS PROPHETARUM, *Naud.*
C. amarus, *Stocks.*
Stocks. Sindh.

505. C. MELO, *L.*
C. Momordica, *Roxb.*
C. utilissimus, *Roxb.*
C. cicatrisatus, *Stocks.*
C. pubescens, *Willd., Mill.*
Edgew. *C. Momordica, Melo,* and *utilissimus,* "Kakri," cult. Multan; *cicatrisatus,* "Albinda," indigenous, Sandal Bar, Multan.
T. T. *C. pubescens* indigenous, Punjab, Rampur, Moradabad; *utilissimus* cult. Punjab, Moradabad.

A. *C. pubescens* indigenous, Jhelum, Hushiarpur; *Melo*, "Kurbooza," Melon, cult. all over Punjab; *utilissimus*, "Kukree," cult. everywhere, Punjab.

Stocks. *C. pubescens* indigenous, Indus basin.

506. C. SATIVUS, *L.*

A. Jhelum, and in all the gardens of the Punjab; the Cucumber, "Keera," is cultivated very commonly also by natives.

507. C. TRIGONUS, *Roxb.*

C. Pseudo-colocynthis, *Royle.*

Royle. Delhi.

Edgew. Punjab; Sandal Bar; Loodiana; Seikh Protected States; Multan.

Frere. Beluch.

508. CITRULLUS COLOCYNTHIS, *Schrd.*

Cucumis Colocynthis, *L.*

Edgew. Multan.

A. Jhelum; Lahore; Umritsur.

T. T. Lahore; Ferozepur; Kussoor.

J. L. S. Peshaur.

Stocks. Sindh.

A. Yields the true Colocynth Gourd.

509. C. VULGARIS, *Schrd.*

C. fistulosus, *Stocks.*

Cucumis Citrullus, *Sering.*

Cucurbita Citrullus, *L.*

Edgew. Punjab, cult.

T. T. Punjab; Lahore.

A. Over the whole Punjab extensively grown, called "Turbooza," Water-melon.

Stocks. Sindh.

510. CEPHALANDRA.

Coccinia indica, *W. & A.*

T. T. Moradabad; Lahore.

Stocks. Indus basin.

511. CUCURBITA PEPO, *L.*

A. Jhelum, cult., "Kuddoo."

512. BRYONIA LACINIOSA, *L.*

T. T. Jamu; Punjab.

513. MUKIA SCABRELLA, *Arn.*

Edgew. Multan.

T. T. Moradabad; Dehra-Dhun; Punjab.

Stocks. Sindh; Beluchistan.

514. **Zehneria.**
Pilogyne cerasiformis, *Stocks.*
Stocks. Sindh ; Indus basin.

515. **Zehneria.**
Pilogyne Garcinii, *Schrad.*
Edgew. Bandelkhand.
Stocks. Deesa ; Sindh.

516. **Corallocarpus epigæus,** *H. f.*
Æchmandra epigæa, *Arn.*
Stocks. Indus basin.

CACTEÆ.

517. **Opuntia Dillenii,** *DC.*
Cactus indica, *Roxb.*
T. T. Lahore.
A. Jhelum ; Tullagung (not in 'Flora of Jhelum') ; Hushiarpur, called "Thor."
Griff. Googerat side of Jhelum river, near Jhelum.

FICOIDEÆ.

518. **Trianthema obcordata,** *Roxb.*
Edgew, Amballa.
T. T. Moradabad ; Lahore ; Meerut.
Falconer. Plains of North-west India.
Stocks. Indus basin ; Sindh.

519. **T. pentandra,** *L.*
T. indica, *Hochst.*
Edgew. Multan ; Thanesar.
T. T. Moradabad ; Lahore ; Ferozepur.
A. Jhelum.
J. L. S. Peshaur.
Stocks. Sindh.
Griff. Afghan.

520. **T. triquetra,** *Roth.*
T. cristallina, *Vahl.*
Edgew. Multan.
T. T. Lahore ; Ferozepur ; Meerut ; Loodiana.
J. L. S. Peshaur.
Stocks. Sindh.

521. **Diplochonium Hochstetteri**, ***Stocks.***
Edgew. **Multan; Jhung.**
Stocks. **Sindh.**

522. **Orygia trianthemoides**, ***Endl.***
O. decumbens, ***Forsk.***
Edgew. **Punjab; Multan; Sha-Kote.**
Jacq. **No. 122 (2358).**
J. L. S. **Peshaur; Attock.**
Vicary. **Boogta Hills.**
Stocks. **Sindh.**

523. **Mollugo cerviana**, ***Ser.***
Edgew. **Multan; Amballa.**
T. T. **Meerut; Punjab; Loodiana.**
A. **Jhelum.**
J. L. S. **Peshaur.**
Vicary. **Ferozepur.**
Stocks. **Sindh.**

524. **M. Glinus**, ***A. Rich.***
Glinus lotoides, ***L.***
Edgew. **Multan; Balanwali.**
T. T. **Moradabad; Lahore; Loodiana; Ferozepur.**
Jacq. **No. 83 (1545).**
A. **Hushiarpur.**
Stocks. **Sindh.**

525. **M. nudicaulis**, ***L.***
Edgew. **Multan; Loodiana.**
T. T. **Punjab; Lahore; Ferozepur; Loodiana.**
A. **Jhelum.**
J. L. S. **Peshaur.**

526. **Gisekia pharnaceoides**, ***L.***
Edgew. **Multan; Amballa.**
T. T. **Delhi; Punjab.**
Stocks. **Sindh.**
Frere. **Beluchistan.**

Var. linearifolia, ***Moq.***
T. T. **Meerut.**
A. **Jhelum.**
J. L. S. **Peshaur.**
Stocks. **Sindh.**

Var. rubella, ***Hochst.***
Edgew. **Multan.**
Stocks. **Sindh (*hb. Edgew.*).**

527. LIMEUM INDICUM, *Stocks.*
Edgew. Lower Punjab; Sirhind; Multan; Jhung.
A. Jhelum.
Stocks. Beluchistan; Sindh.

UMBELLIFERÆ.

528. HYDROCOTYLE ASIATICA, *L.*
T. T. Moradabad; Jamu; Punjab.
A. Jhelum.

529. ERYNGIUM CÆRULEUM, *Bieb.*
J. L. S. Peshaur; Hazara.

530. PYCNOCYCLA GLAUCA, *Royle.*
Royle. Banks of the Sutlej.

531. BUPLEURUM FALCATUM, *L.*
J. L. S. Hazara.

532. APIUM GRAVEOLENS, *L.*
Edgew. Gardens, Umballa.
A. Indigenous, Jhelum; Kulaka-har.
Stocks. Beluchistan.
Griff. Afghan.
A. Cult. in the gardens of Europeans. Celery.

533. PETROSELINUM SATIVUM, *Hoff.*
Edgew. Umballa, gardens; Multan. Parsley.
A. Cultivated by Europeans.

534. CARUM COPTICUM, *Benth.*
Ptychotis coptica, *DC.*
P. Ajowan, *W. & A.*
Edgew. Multan.
T. T. Punjab, cultivated.
A. Jhelum.

535. SIUM ANGUSTIFOLIUM, *L.*
J. L. S. Peshaur.

536. PIMPINELLA ANISUM, *L.*
A. Jhelum, spread perhaps from cultivation.

537. PSAMMOGETON BITERNATUM, *Edgew.*
Pimpinella crinita, *Boiss.*
Edgew. Umballa.

T. T. Ferozepur ; Loodiana ; Jamu.
Fleming. Salt range.
A. Jhelum ; Hushiarpur.
Vicary. Peshaur.
J. L. S. Hazara ; Peshaur.
J. Young, Hb. Edgew. Attock.

538. SCANDIX PECTEN-VENERIS, *L.*
T. T. Jamu Hills, 5000 ft. ; Kashmir.
J. L. S. Hazara.
Stocks. Beluchistan.
Griff. Afghan.

539. FŒNICULUM VULGARE, *L.*
F. panmorium, *DC.*
T. T. Punjab, cult.
A. Jhelum, from cultivation.

540. ŒNANTHE STOLONIFERA, *Wall.*
Œ. corticata, *Edgew.*
Edgew. Radaur ; Delhi canal.
T. T. Moradabad.
J. L. S. Peshaur.

541. PEUCEDANUM.
Anethum graveolens, *L.*
A. Sowa, *Roxb.*
Edgew. Multan ; Amballa, cult.
J. L. S. Peshaur, cult.
Stocks. Sindh ; Beluchistan.
Griff. Afghan.

542. CORIANDRUM SATIVUM, *L.*
Edgew. Multan ; Amballa, cult.
T. T. Cult. largely, Punjab.
A. Jhelum.
J. L. S. Peshaur.

543. CUMINUM CYMINUM, *L.*
T. T. Ferozepur, an escape.
A. Jhelum, cult. and escape.

544. DAUCUS CAROTA, *L.*
T. T. Punjab, cult. ; Kashmir, indigenous.
A. Cult. as a garden crop very largely, round towns, in the Punjab. Called "Gauger," Carrot.

545. **Caucalis leptophylla**, *L.*
Vicary. Peshaur.
Stocks. Beluchistan.
Griff. Afghan.

546. **Caucalis.**
Torilis nodosa, *L.*
A. Jhelum.
Griff. Afghan.

ARALIACEÆ.

547. **Heptapleurum venulosum**, *Benth.*
Edgew. Tikoli valley.
St. & Wint. Kumaon, 3000 ft.
A. Hushiarpur, gardens.

CORNACEÆ.

548. **Alangium hexapetalum**, *Lam.*, var. **decapetalum**, *Vahl.*
Edgew. Sub Sewaliks ; Isaferabad.
Royle. North-west India ; banks of the Jumna.

549. **Marlea begoniæfolia**, *Roxb.*
Royle. Further north than 30° north latitude.
Edgew. Deobun.
T. T. Kumaon ; Simla.
St. & Wint. Kumaon.

MONOPETALÆ.

LORANTHACEÆ.

550. **Loranthus longiflorus**, *Desr.*
L. bicolor, *Roxb.*
T. T. Kumaon ; Rohilkund.
St. & Wint. Kumaon.
A. Hushiarpur, parasitical on *Acacia Lebbek* and *Flacourtia sapida* ; native name "Purnd."

RUBIACEÆ.

a. Cinchoneæ.

551. Borreria lasiocarpa, *W. & A.*
T. T. Jamu; Moradabad.
A. Jhelum; Hushiarpur.

552. Spermacoce articularis, *L.*, var. hispida, *H. f. & T.*
S. hispida, *L.*
Edgew. Loodiana.
T. T. Moradabad to Delhi; Kumaon; Simla.
A. Hushiarpur.

553. Gaillonia hymenostephana, *Jb. et Sp.*
Fleming. Punjab.
Stocks. Beluchistan.

554. Morinda tinctoria, *Roxb.*
Edgew. Amballa.

555. Hamiltonia suaveolens, *Roxb.*
T. T. Simla.
Fleming. Salt range.
A. Jhelum; Hushiarpur Hills.

556. Leptodermis virgata, *Edgew. MS.*
Fleming. Punjab; Salt range; Dunna Hill.
Falconer. Dhurm-toar; Indus, above Attock.

557. Hedyotis aspera, *Heyne.*
A. Jhelum; Punjab.
Stocks. Indus basin.

558. H. brachypoda, *DC.*
Royle. North-west India.
T. T. Moradabad.

559. H. Burmanniana, *Br.*
Edgew. Multan.
T. T. Jamu; Moradabad.
A. Hushiarpur.

560. Wendlandia exserta, *DC.*
W. cinerea, *Wall.*
Edgew. Multan, seeds carried down by the river; Jhung.

T. T. Kumaon.
St. & Wint. Kumaon, 3000 ft.
A. Hushiarpur.

561. HYMENODICTYON EXCELSUM, *Wall.*
St. & Wint. Kumaon, 2500 ft.
Jacq. (Where ?)
A. Hushiarpur; Purwain Forest, common.

562. NAUCLEA PARVIFOLIA, *Roxb.*
T. T. Moradabad; Kumaon to Delhi.
A. Hushiarpur, indigenous; is not an uncommon cultivated tree in the Punjab.

563. RANDIA LONGISPINA, *DC.*, and var. DUMETORUM.
R. dumetorum, *Lam.*
Royle. North-western India.
T. T. Moradabad.
A. Hushiarpur, a common jungle shrub, bearing a fruit likely to be mistaken for a small apple; the fruit called "Mine-phul;" the shrub "Arara." The fruit is sold in large quantities in Umritsur, and used as an emetic by the natives.

564. GARDENIA TETRASPERMA, *Roxb.*
Munro. Sewaliks.
Edgew. Sewaliks.
A. Jhelum: Salt range.

b. GALIEÆ.

565. GALIUM APARINE, *L.*
A. Jhelum; Hushiarpur.
Vicary. Attock.
J. L. S. Peshaur.

566. G. PAUCIFLORUM, *Bunge.*
Fleming. Salt range.

567. G. TRICORNE, *With.*
J. L. S. Peshaur (?).
Stocks. Beluchistan.
Griff. Afghan.

568. RUBIA TINCTORIA, *L.*
Stocks. Sindh, cult.
Griff. Afghan., cult.

569. ASPERULA CYNANCHICA, *L.*
St. & Wint. Garwhal; Niti, 11,500 ft.
J. L. S. Peshaur.

DIPSACACEÆ.

570. **Scabiosa Olivieri**, *Coult.*
J. Young, herb. Edgew. Attock, No. 4063.
Vicary. Peshaur.
J. L. S. Peshaur.
Stocks. Beluchistan.
Griff. Afghan.

COMPOSITÆ.

571. **Vernonia anthelmintica**, *Willd.*
T. T. Lahore; Kalka, "doubtful if truly wild."

572. **V. cinerea**, *Less.*
Edgew. Multan.
T. T. Moradabad; Jamu; Lahore.
Lady Dalhousie. Karnál.
A. Jhelum.

573. **Vernonia**, species.
No. 39, *Hb. H. f. & T. T.*
Fleming. Salt range.
Vicary. Peshaur.
Frere. Beluchistan.

574. **Vernonia**, species.
No. 32, *Hb. Hook. fil. & T. T.*
Fleming. Salt range.
Vicary. Peshaur.

575. **Adenostemma elatum**, *Don.*
T. T. Punjab; Jamu; Kalka.
Fleming. Marri.
J. L. S. Peshaur (species?).

576. **Poloa**, species.
Stocks, No. 590. Sindh; Beluch.
Vicary. Sindh; Boogta Hills.

577. **Erigeron canadensis**, *L.*
T. T. Moradabad and Himalaya, introduced.
A. Jhelum, quite naturalized.

578. **Linosyris tatarica**, *Meyer.*
Vicary. Boogta Hills.

579. GRANGEA MADRASPATANA, *Poir.*
G. ægyptiaca, *DC.*
Edgew. No. 5008. Multan.
Royle. Delhi.
T. T. Moradabad.
Stocks. Sindh.

580. CYATHOCLINE LYRATA, *Cass.*
Edgew. Radaur.
T. T. Moradabad; Seharanpur; Jamu.

581. SPHÆRANTHUS HIRTUS, *Willd.*
Edgew. Banda; Sewaliks; Khizerabad.
T. T. Meerut; Moradabad; Lahore.

582. BERTHELOTIA LANCEOLATA, *DC.*
B. indica, *DC.*
Edgew. Multan.
T. T. Ferozepur; Lahore.
A. Jhelum.
J. L. S. Peshaur.
Vicary. Sindh.
Stocks. Sindh.
Griff. Afghan.

583. CONYZA ABSINTHIFOLIA, *DC.*
Edgew. Amballa.
T. T. Bari-Doab; Jamu plains.
A. Jhelum.

584. C. ÆGYPTIACA, *Ait.*
C. sublyrata, *Wight.*
T. T. Moradabad; Jalinder; Ferozepur; Loodiana.

585. C. BOVEI, *Decais.*
Stocks. Sindh.

586. C. RUFA, *Wall.*
C. marginata, *Edgew.*
T. T. Moradabad; Loodiana.
Edgew. Loodiana.

587. C. VISCIDULA, *Wall.*
C. polycephala, *Edgew.*
Royle. North-west India.
Edgew. Dadūpūr; Hurdwar.
T. T. Moradabad.

588. C. VERONICÆFOLIA, *Wall.*
T. T. Chenab; Jamu plains.
Griff. Afghan.

589. PHAGNALON DENTICULATUM, *DC.*
Vicary. Mar-gulla pass (near Rhotas, Jhelum).
T. T. Jamu.
J. L. S. Peshaur.
Griff. Afghan.

590. BLUMEA AURITA, *DC.*
T. T. Moradabad; Meerut; Lahore.
Stocks. Sindh.

591. B. OXYODONTA, *DC.*
Edgew. Banda.
T. T. Moradabad; Jamu.

592. B. RUNCINATA, *DC.*
T. T. Lahore; Sealkote.

593. B. WIGHTIANA, *DC.*
B. lacera, *DC.*
Edgew. Amballa.
T. T. Lahore; Jalinder; Loodiana.
A. Jhelum.
J. L. S. Peshaur.

594. PLUCHEA DIOSCORIDIS, *DC.*
J. L. S. Western Punjab.

595. P. OVALIS, *DC.*
A. Salt range, large shrub. No. 392.

596. PLUCHEA, sp.
No. 1, *H. f. & T.*, distribution.
A. No. 384. Salt range.
Vicary. Boogta Hills.
Stocks. Sindh. No. 553.
Dalzel. Sindh? (44).

597. P. WALLICHIANA, *DC.*
T. T. Loodiana.
Stocks. Beluchistan. No. 627.

598. INULA CAPPA, *DC.*
A. Hushiarpur.

599. I. EUPATORIOIDES, *DC.*
T. T. Jamu; Simla.
J. L. S. Peshaur.

600. I. GRAVEOLENS, *Desf.*
J. L. S. Peshaur.
Griff. Afghan.

601. I. VESTITA, *Wall.*
T. T. Lahore; Ferozepur; Moradabad; Loodiana.
A. Jhelum; Hushiarpur.

602. VICOA INDICA, *Wight.*
T. T. Lahore; Loodiana; banks of Chenab; Rechnab-Doab; Jamu.
Vicary. Ferozepur.
A. Hushiarpur.

603. PENTANEMA DIVARICATUM, *Cass.*
Stocks. Sindh, *hb. Edgew.*

604. FRANCŒURIA CRISPA, *Cass.*
Edgew. Multan; Balanwali.
T. T. Lahore; Ferozepur; banks of Chenab.
A. Jhelum.
J. L. S. Peshaur.
Stocks. Sindh; Beluchistan.

605. PULICARIA VULGARIS, *Gaert.*
P. arabica, *Cass.*
J. L. S. Peshaur.
Stocks. Indus basin.
Jacq. No. 1069.

606. P. SAXICOLA, *Edgew.*
Edgew. Banda.
Royle. North-west Provinces.
Stocks. Sindh.

607. CÆSULIA AXILLARIS, *Roxb.*
T. T. Moradabad; Rechnab Doab; Jamu plains; Kalka.
A. Hushiarpur.

608. ECLIPTA ERECTA, *L.*
E. prostrata, *L.*
Edgew. Multan.
T. T. Ravee Doab; Lahore; Ferozepur; Moradabad.
A. Jhelum; Hushiarpur.
J. L. S. Peshaur.
Stocks. Sindh.
Griff. Afghan.

609. BLAINVILLEA LATIFOLIA, *DC.*
B. alba, *Edgew.*
Edgew. Pinjor-Dhun.
T. T. Banks of Chenab; Amballa; Kalka.
A. Jhelum.
Stocks. Sindh; Beluchistan.

610. Xanthium strumarium, *L.*
X. indicum, *Roxb.*
Edgew. Multan.
T. T. Lahore; Rowlee-Ghat; Moradabad.
A. Jhelum.
J. L. S. Peshaur.
Stocks. Indus basin.

611. Sclerocarpus africanus, *Jacq.*
Edgew. Banda.
T. T. Kalka.
A. Jhelum.

612. Helianthus tuberosus, *L.*
Edgew. Amballa, hort.
A. The Jerusalem Artichoke is only cultivated for Europeans, as is the *Cynara Scolymus,* L., the common Artichoke.

613. Bidens bipinnata, *L.*
B. decomposita, *Wall.*
T. T. Moradabad; banks of the Sutlej.
A. Jhelum.

614. B. cernua, *L.*
T. T. Kashmir.
J. L. S. Peshaur.

615. B. Wallichii, *DC.*
Stocks. Under 4000 feet, Beluchistan.

616. Cosmos sulphureus, *Cav.*
T. T. Moradabad, cultiv. frequent.

617. Chrysanthellum indicum, *DC.*
Edgew. Banda.
T. T. Moradabad.

618. Tagetes erecta, *L.*
Edgew. Hort. Amballa. Cultivated from the tropics to the highest Himalayan village, "Gendha."
A. Cultivated in every garden in the Punjab.

619. T. patula, *L.*
Edgew. Hort. Amballa.

620. Anthemis odontostephana, *Boiss.*
Vicary. Peshaur.
Griff. Afghan. No. 3189, distrib.
Stocks. Beluchistan.

621. ACHILLÆA MILLEFOLIUM, *L.*
T. T. Kumaon.
Lady Dalhousie. Simla.
Fleming. Marri.
J. L. S. (Species ?) Peshaur.

622. A. SANTOLINA, *L.*
Stocks. Beluchistan.
Griff. Afghan.

623. MATRICARIA CHAMOMILLA, *L.*
M. suaveolens, *L.*
T. T. Lahore; Meerut; Moradabad.
Edgew. Amballa.

624. M. DISCIFORMIS, *DC.*
J. L. S. Peshaur.
Griff. Afghan.

625. MATRICARIA.
No. 3, *H. f. & T. Herb.* "Near *præcox*, DC."
Vicary. Peshaur.
J. L. S. Peshaur.
Stocks. Beluch.
Griff. Afghan.

626. CHRYSANTHEMUM CORONARIUM, *L.*
T. T. Moradabad; Ferozepur; Meerut, always cultivated.

627. ARTEMISIA SACRORUM, *Led.*
A. laciniata, *Willd.*
T. T. Thibet, 8000 to 12,000 feet.
J. L. S. Peshaur.

628. A. SCOPARIA, *Wal. & Kt.*
A. elegans, *Roxb.*
Edgew. Amballa; Loodiana.
T. T. Moradabad; west of Chenab; east of Lahore.
A. Jhelum; Hushiarpur.
J. L. S. Peshaur.

629. A. VESTITA, *Wall.*
J. L. S. Peshaur.

630. A. VULGARIS, *L.*
A. indica, *Willd.*
J. L. S. Peshaur.
Fleming. Chumba.

631. **Myriogyne minuta**, *Less.*
Edgew. Multan; Khizerabad.
T. T. Meerut; Jamu plains; Ferozepur.
A. Hushiarpur.
Royle. North-west provinces of India, "Nuk-chinknee" (Sneeze-wort). The same name applied to it in the Hushiarpur district.

632. **Machlis hemisphærica**, *DC.*
Cotula anthemoides, *L.*
Plerogyne Cardiospermum, *Edgew.*
Royle. Sup. Gangetic plain; Delhi.
Edgew. Khizerabad.
T. T. Moradabad; Ferozepur; Lahore.
A. Jhelum; Hushiarpur.

633. **Pterochæta**, sp.
Fleming. North of Salt range.
Stocks, No. 437. Beluchistan.

634. **Gnaphalium indicum**, *L.*
G. niliacum, *Spreng.*
A. By all collectors everywhere, *T. T.*, *Edgew.*, *Royle*, *Stocks*, *Griffith*, *J. L. S.*, *A.*

635. **G. luteo-album**, *DC.*
G. pallidum, *Wall.*
Edgew. Loodiana.
T. T. Lahore; east of Ferozepur; Jalinder; Moradabad.
A. Jhelum.
Vicary. Peshaur.
Stocks. Beluchistan.
Frere. Beluchistan.
Griff. Afghan.

636. **G. multiceps**, *Wall.*
T. T. Ferozepur; Moradabad.
Griff. Afghan.
J. L. S. Peshaur.

637. **Lasiopogon muscoides**, *DC.*
Vicary. Peshaur.
Griff. Afghan.

638. **Filago germanica**, *L.*
Gnaphalium Hardwaricum, *Wall.*
G. prostratum, *DC.*
T. T. Moradabad; Ferozepur; Meerut; Lahore.
Fleming. Salt range.

A. Jhelum; Hushiarpur.
J. L. S. Peshaur.
Edgew. Jagadhri; Loodiana; Thanesar.
Griff. Afghan.

639. TRICHOGYNE CAULIFLORA, *DC.*
Edgew. Radaur; Multan.
T. T. East of Ferozepur; Meerut; Loodiana; Moradabad.
Jacq. Punjab.
A. Jhelum; Hushiarpur.
J. L. S. Peshaur.
Stocks. Beluchistan; Sindh.

640. EMILIA SAGITTATA, *DC.*
T. T. Moradabad.

641. E. SONCHIFOLIA, *DC.*
Edgew. Pinjor-Dhun; Kajurwale.
T. T. Moradabad; Meerut; Kumaon; Shahabad.
Jacq. Agra.

642. SENECIO CORONOPIFOLIUS, *Desf.*
T. T. Jamu, 4000 to 8000 ft.
Vicary. Peshaur.
Stocks. Beluchistan.
Griff. Afghan.

643. CALENDULA OFFICINALIS, *L.*
T. T. Hort. Ferozepur.
Vicary. Peshaur.
J. L. S. Peshaur.
Griff. Afghan.

644. ECHINOPS ECHINATUS, *Roxb.*
Edgew. Multan.
T. T. Lahore.
A. Jhelum.
Stocks. Sindh.

645. APLOTAXIS ALBESCENS, *DC.*
Edgew. Loodiana; Khizerabad.

646. A. CANDICANS, *DC.*
A. scaposa, *Edgew.*
T. T. Jamu; Lahore.
A. Jhelum; Hushiarpur.
Fleming. Salt range.
J. L. S. Peshaur.
Jacq. Punjab; Agra.

647. Cousinia calcitrapæformis, *Jb. et Sp.*
A. Jhelum (omitted in 'Flora of Jhelum District'), common.
Vicary. Peshaur.
J. L. S. Peshaur.
J. Young, hb. Edgew. Attock.
Griff. Afghan.
Stocks. Beluch.

648. Amberboa odorata, *DC.*
T. T. Cult. hort. Ferozepur.
Stocks. Sindh. No. 1154.

649. Microlonchus divaricatus, *DC.*
Serratula divaricata, *F. & M.*
Edgew. Multan.
T. T. Moradabad; Ferozepur; Loodiana; Lahore.
Stocks. Sindh.
Griff. Afghan.

650. Centaurea Calcitrapa, *L.*
T. T. Kashmir.
A. Jhelum; Salt range.
Fleming. Marri; Salt range.
J. L. S. Peshaur.
Stocks. Beluch.
Griff. Afghan.

651. C. cyanus, *L.*
A. Jhelum, perhaps introduced in corn-seed.

652. Carthamus oxyacantha, *Bieb.*
Edgew. Multan; Amballa.
T. T. Lahore; Jalinder Doab; Ferozepur; Sealkote.
A. Jhelum (omitted in 'Flora of Jhelum'), common.
J. L. S. Peshaur, "oil extracted from its seeds, used as food; seeds eaten parched."

653. C. tinctorius, *L.*
A. Cultivated generally throughout the Punjab for its florets, from which a dye is extracted. The plant called "Kussoomba," Safflower. An oil is occasionally extracted from its seed. Moradabad; Punjab; Sindh; Kabul.

654. Silybum marianum, *Gaert.*
Edgew. Deena-Nugur (Punjab).
T. T. Jamu.
J. L. S. Peshaur.
Griff. Hb. Benth.

655. CIRSIUM ARVENSE, *Scop.*
Edgew. Multan; Amballa.
T. T. Punjab; Himalaya and Thibet.
J. L. S. Peshaur.

656. C. WALLICHII, *DC.*
Royle. Jumna.
T. T. Jamu, 6000 feet.
Jacq. Dehra-Dhun; Kumaon.

657. JURINEA MODESTA, *Boiss.*
Vicary ?. Peshaur.

658. DICOMA TOMENTOSA, *Cass.*
D. lanuginosa, *DC.*
Royle. Delhi.
Stocks. Sindh.

659. KÖLPINIA LINEARIS, *Pallas.*
Vicary. Peshaur.
J. L. S. Peshaur.
Stocks. Beluch.

660. CICHORIUM ENDIVIA, *L.*
Edgew. Hort. Umballa.
T. T. Lahore, cult.

661. C. INTYBUS, *L.*
Edgew. Multan, cult.
A. Jhelum, cult. common garden-weed, used as a pot-herb; Hushiarpur.
J. L. S. Peshaur.
Stocks. Beluchistan.
Griff. Afghan.

662. SCORZONERA RAMOSISSIMA, *Boiss.*
Stocks. Beluchistan to Kurrachee, 4000 ft. No. 1161 of Stocks's list (named *S. subaphylla*, Boiss.) is referred in Kew herb. to this.

663. PICRIDIUM TINGITANUM, *Desf.*
A. Jhelum, cultivated always.
Jacq. Punjab.
Stocks. Beluchistan.
Griff. Afghan.

664. SONCHUS ARVENSIS, *L.*
T. T. Jamu plains.
Fleming. Salt range.
A. Jhelum.
J. L. S. Peshaur.

665. S. ASPER, *Fuchs.*
T. T. Lahore; Moradabad.
A. Jhelum.
Stocks. Beluchistan; Sindh.

666. S. CANDOLLEANUS, *Jb. et Sp.*
Psammoseris divaricata, *Edgew.*
Edgew. Northern India; Multan; Balanwali; Adunwan.
Jacq. Punjab.
Stocks. Sindh.

667. S. OLERACEUS, *L.*
S. ciliatus, *Lam.*
Edgew. Amballa; Multan.
T. T. Lahore; Meerut; Moradabad.
J. L. S. Peshaur.
Stocks. Sindh.

668. YOUNGIA THUNBERGIANA, *DC.*
Y. runcinata, *DC.*
Edgew. Khizerabad; Dūnpūr.
T. T. Plains below Jamu.
A. Hushiarpur.

669. PHÆNOPUS VIMINEUS, *Rch.*
Stocks. Beluch.
Griff. Afghan.
J. L. S. Peshaur.

670. LACTUCA AURICULATA, *DC.*
L. arvensis, *Edgew.*
T. T. Jalinder.
A. Jhelum.
J. L. S. Peshaur.

671. L. SATIVA, *L.*
Edgew. Cultivated, Multan; Amballa.
T. T. Cultivated, Moradabad; Ladak.
A. The Lettuce is cultivated commonly in the Punjab, by the natives, "to whom it seems to have been a garden-vegetable independent of European introduction."

672. TARAXACUM DENS-LEONIS, *Desf.*
Edgew. At Amb in the Hushiarpur district in profusion, also Adinanuggūr.
J. L. S. Peshaur.

673. MICRORHYNCHUS ASPLENIIFOLIUS, *DC.*
Edgew. Amballa.
T. T. Lahore; Ferozepur; Moradabad.

674. M. NUDICAULIS, *Less.*
M. patens, *DC.*
Edgew. Multan; Amballa.
T. T. Moradabad; west of Chenab; east of Ferozepur; Loodiana; Lahore.
Jacq. Agra.
A. Jhelum.
J. L. S. Peshaur.
Stocks. Sindh; Beluch.
Griff. Afghan.

675. M. SARMENTOSUS, *DC.*
Edgew. Multan.
Stocks. Indus basin.

CAMPANULACEÆ.

676. WAHLENBERGIA AGRESTIS, *A. DC.*
W. dehiscens, *A. DC.*
Edgew. Loodiana.
T. T. Moradabad; Garwhal; Kumaon.
A. Hushiarpur, its (as yet) most north-west range.

677. CAMPANULA CANESCENS, *Wall.*
Edgew. Punjab; Loodiana; Khizerabad.
T. T. Lahore; Moradabad.
Vicary. Amballa.
A. Jhelum; Mt. Tilla; Hushiarpur.
Griff. Afghan.

SPHENOCLEACEÆ.

678. SPHENOCLEA ZEYLANICA, *Gaert.*
Pongatium indicum, *Lam.*
T. T. Punjab; Moradabad; Lahore.
Edgew. Multan.

GOODENIACEÆ.

679. SCÆVOLA PLUMIERI, *Vahl.*
S. uvifera, *Stocks.*
Vicary. Sindh (sea-shore).
Stocks. Sindh (sea-shore).

LOBELIACEÆ.

680. **Lobelia trigona**, *Roxb.*
H. f. & T. Throughout all India from Burmah to Simla to 6000 feet.

PLUMBAGINACEÆ.

681. **Statice Stocksii**, *Bois.*
Stocks. Sindh (probably sea-shore).

682. **Plumbago zeylanica**, *L.*
Royle. North-west India.
Edgew. Multan; Jagadhri.
T. T. Punjab; Moradabad.
A. Jhelum.
Fleming. Punjab.
Stocks. Beluchistan.

PRIMULACEÆ.

683. **Samolus Valerandi**, *L.*
T. T. Rampur.
A. Jhelum.
J. L. S. Peshaur.
Vicary. Peshaur.
Stocks. Beluchistan.
Griff. Afghan.

684. **Androsace rotundifolia**, *L.*
Edgew. Khizerabad.
T. T. Moradabad; Hurdwar.
A. Jhelum; Hushiarpur.
Vicary. Amballa.

685. **Anagallis arvensis**, *L.*, var. **cærulea.**
Edgew. Multan.
T. T. Punjab.
A. Jhelum; Umritsur; Hushiarpur.
J. L. S. Peshaur.
Stocks. Indus basin.
J. L. S. "Is always blue in the Punjab, and red in Kashmir."

MYRSINACEÆ.

686. **Myrsine.**
M. africana, *L.*
M. bifaria, *Wall.*
Royle. North-west-India hills.
T. T. Nyne-Tal; Kumaon.
J. L. S. Peshaur.
Griff. Afghan.

687. **Ægiceras majus**, *Gaert.*
Stocks. Sindh; Indus basin.

688. **Reptonia buxifolia**, *A. DC.*
Edgeworthia buxifolia, *Falc.*
Edgew. hb. from W. G. Peshaur.
J. L. S. Peshaur.
Griff. Afghan.
J. L. S. "Helps to form the shrubby vegetation of the Peshaur valley. Its fruit 'Gur-gura.'"

SAPOTACEÆ.

689. **Bassia latifolia**, *Roxb.*
Edgew. Amballa (cult. ?).
A. Hushiarpur, both cultivated and apparently indigenous. I never met with it in any other part of the Punjab.
Called "Mahwah."

690. **Mimusops Elengi**, *L.*
A. Cultivated and uncommon in the Punjab.
Edgew. Multan, cult.
A. Called "Morsre," "Moulseri."
Edgew. Called "Mūlsri," Hind.

691. **M. indica**, *DC.*
M. hexandra, *Wight, non Roxb.*
M. Kauki, *Wall., non L.*
Edgew. Banda, indigenous; Multan, cult.
T. T. Moradabad, cult.
A. Cultivated and uncommon, Hushiarpur; Philor, "Kirnee." The fruit eaten; it gives the best shade of any tree I know in India.

EBENACEÆ.

692. **Diospyros cordifolia**, *Roxb.*
Edgew. Amballa; Pinjor-Dhun.
Royle. Monghir.
T. T. Moradabad.
A. Hushiarpur; Gūrdaspur, a common tree-shrub, called "Hirreck."

693. **D. Lotus**, *L.*
Griff. Afghan.
J. L. S. The fruit is brought from the hills to the town; the tree does not grow near Peshaur. Called "Amlok."

694. **Diospyros.**
D. melanoxylon, *Roxb.*
Royle. Banda.
A. Hushiarpur; Madhapur; Gūrdaspur, low hills, a characteristic shrub (seldom a tree), called "Kinnoo." The fruit is eaten in a decayed state, and is largely sold in the Umritsur market.

695. **D. montana**, *Roxb.*
Royle. North-west Provinces of India.
Edgew. Banda.

OLEACEÆ.

696. **Olea europæa**, *L.*, var.
O. cuspidata, *Wall.*
O. ferruginea, *Wall.*
A. Jhelum; Mt. Tilla; Salt range; Hushiarpur, only one, but an immense tree, on the road to Gūgrate, in the Choa under the second Thanna from Hushiarpur; I am sorry I never took the measurement of this tree. A variety of the European Olive, and called in the Salt range and Jhelum district "Cow."
Fleming. Salt range.
J. L. S. Peshaur.
Stocks. Beluchistan; Sindh.
Griff. Afghan., cultivated.

JASMINACEÆ.

697. Jasminum arborescens, *Roxb.*
J. latifolium, *Wight.*
Edgew. Near San-Sadhaura.
T. T. Cult. Lahore; Kumaon.
St. & Wint. Kumaon, 3000 ft.

698. J. auriculatum, *Vahl.*
T. T. Moradabad; Lahore; Jamu.
A. Hushiarpur.

699. J. grandiflorum, *L.*
T. T. Cult. Lahore.
A. Jhelum; Hushiarpur, certainly not from cultivation.

700. J. pubescens, *Willd.*
T. T. Kumaon; Rohilkhand.
St. & Wint. Kumaon, 1000 ft.
A. Hushiarpur jungles, not uncommon.

701. J. quinqueflorum, *Heyne.*
T. T. Moradabad; Garwhal.

702. J. revolutum, *Sims*, var. β. pubigerum.
T. T. Simla; Kumaon.
St. & W. Kumaon.
J. L. S. Peshaur.
Griff. Afghan.

703. Nyctanthes arbor-tristis, *L.*
Edgew. Pinjor-Dhun, abundant.
T. T. Upper India, indigenous; Bijnore; Kumaon.
St. & Wint. Kumaon, 2500 ft.
A. Cultivated in every garden in the Punjab, called "Harsingar;" met with it in the Purwain range of hills, Hushiarpur, where I thought it an escape; but it must have been indigenous.

APOCYNACEÆ.

704. Carissa Carandas, *L.*
T. T. Cult. Meerut; Moradabad.
A. Cult. Punjab gardens; not common at Jhelum, Lahore, Umritsur. The fruit used in tarts, called "Karounda."

705. C. **DIFFUSA**, ***Roxb.***
Royle. **North-west India.**
T. T. **Moradabad; Punjab.**
A. **Jhelum; Hushiarpur, "Gurna:" fruit eaten and very good, but small.**
Fleming. **Salt range.**

706. **OPHIOXYLON SERPENTINUM**, ***Willd.***
T. T. **Moradabad.**
Edgew. **Bilaspur.**

707. **THEVETIA NERIIFOLIA**, ***Juss.***
Royle. **North-west India.**
T. T. **Cult. Moradabad; Meerut.**
A. **Cult. tree throughout the gardens of the Punjab.**

708. **TABERNÆMONTANA CORONARIA**, ***R. Br.***
Royle. **North-west India.**
T. T. **Moradabad.**
St. & Wint. **Kumaon.**

709. **VINCA PUSILLA**, ***Murr.***
Royle. **North-west India.**
T. T. **Rampur; Moradabad.**

710. **V. ROSEA**, ***L.***
Royle. **North-west India, cult.**
T. T. **Meerut; Moradabad, cult.**

711. **RHAZYA STRICTA**, ***Decaisne.***
A. **Jhelum.**
Fleming. **Salt range.**
Vicary. **Boogta Hills; Hala Mts.; Sindh.**
J. L. S. **Peshaur.**
Stocks. **Sindh.**
Frere. **Beluchistan.**
Griff. **Afghan.**

712. **PLUMIERA ACUMINATA**, ***Ait.***
A. **Cult. Hushiarpur.**

713. **VALLARIS DICHOTOMA**, ***Wall.***
Royle. **North-west India.**
Edgew. **Sadhaura; Kalesar-Dhun.**
T. T. **Moradabad; Meerut.**
A. **Hushiarpur, "Doodlee."**

714. **HOLARRHENA PUBESCENS**, ***Wall.***
Edgew. **Khizerabad, "Kuori."**

715. NERIUM ODORUM, *Soland.*
Edgew. Multan.
T. T. Moradabad; Lahore; Jamu.
A. Jhelum; Hushiarpur.
Fleming. Salt range; Kew-rah.
J. L. S. Peshaur.
Stocks. Sindh.
Griff. Afghan.
Jacq. Punjab.

716. ICHNOCARPUS FRUTESCENS, *Br.*
Edgew. Sadhaura.
T. T. Moradabad; Rowlee Ghat.
Jacq. North-west India.
A. Hushiarpur, " Buker-bael."

ASCLEPIADACEÆ.

717. PERGULARIA PALLIDA, *W. & A.*
Edgew. Loodiana; Pinjor-Dhun.
T. T. Punjab; Moradabad; Lahore.
J. L. S. Peshaur.

718. ORTHANTHERA VIMINEA, *Wight.*
Edgew. Kalesar-Dhun.
Royle. Kala-doonga.
T. T. North-west India.
St. & Wint. Kumaon.
J. L. S. Peshaur.

719. LEPTADENIA JACQUEMONTII, *Decais.*
Edgew. Multan.
Stocks. Sindh.
Vicary. Sindh.

720. L. RETICULATA, *W. & A.*
Edgew. Amballa.

721. L. SPARTIUM, *Wight.*
Royle. Jumna; North-west India.
T. T. Gurmakesar Ghat.

722. MASTOSTIGMA VARIANS, *Stocks.*
Stocks. Sindh.
Frere. Beluchistan.

723. **Ceropegia bulbosa**, *Roxb.*
T. T. Lahore; Punjab.

724. **C. esculenta**, *Edgew.*
Edgew. Multan.
Stocks. Sindh.

725. **Boucerosia Aucheri**, *Decaisne.*
A. Jhelum, "Chunga."
Fleming. Salt range, "Chunga."
Stocks. Beluchistan.
J. L. S. Peshaur?

726. **B. edulis**, *Edegw.*
Edgew. Multan.
Stocks. Sindh.

727. **Cryptostegia grandiflora**, *Br.*
Edgew. Hort. Amballa.
Royle. North-west India.
T. T. Moradabad; Meerut.
A. Only cultivated in the Punjab.

728. **Hemidesmus indicus**, *Br.*
Royle. Jumna; North-west India.

729. **Periploca aphylla**, *Decaisne.*
Edgew. Multan; Chandnot.
A. Jhelum.
Vicary. Mar-gulla Pass.
Fleming. Salt range.
Jacq. Salt range.
Stocks. Sindh.
Griff. Afghan.

730. **Vincetoxicum luridum**, *Stocks, MS.*
Hb. Stocks, No. 721. Beluchistan to Kurrachee.

731. **Calotropis procera**, *Br.*
C. Hamiltonii, *Wight., Ic.*
Edgew. Multan; Amballa.
T. T. Lahore; east of Fezorepur; Moradabad.
A. Jhelum; Hushiarpur; Umritsur; Philor; Gūrdaspur; Sindh.
J. L. S. Peshaur.
Stocks. Sindh.
Griff. Afghan.

732. **Pentatropis spiralis**, *Decaisne.*
(The dry-country plant is this, and not *P. microphylla,* W. & A. See 'Flora Mallica,' *Edgew.*)

Royle. North-west India.
Edgew. Multan; Loodiana; Amballa.
T. T. Lahore.
A. Jhelum.
Stocks. Sindh.
J. L. S. Peshaur.

733. Oxystelma esculentum, *Br.*
Edgew. Multan.
T. T. Lahore; Chenab.
J. L. S. Peshaur.
A. Sindh; Indus.
Stocks. Sindh.

734. Dæmia cordata, *Br.*
Vicary. Hatu range.
Stocks. Beluchistan.

735. D. extensa, *R. Br.*
Edgew. Multan; Pinjor-Dhun.
T. T. Jamu.
Jacq. Punjab.
Fleming. Salt range; Kew-tha.
A. Jhelum; Hushiarpur.
J. L. S. Peshaur.
Stocks. Indus basin.

SALVADORACEÆ.

736. Salvadora oleoides, *Decaisne.*
S. indica, *hb. Royle.*
Royle. Delhi.
Edgew. Multan; Amballa.
T. T. Punjab; Delhi.
Vicary. Delhi; Ferozepur.
A. Jhelum; Philor; Sindh; Sukker.
Stocks. Indus basin.

737. S. persica, *L.*
Edgew. Multan; Pat-putan.
T. T. Delhi.
Vicary. Delhi.
Madden. Punjab to Patna.

GENTIANACEÆ.

738. GENTIANA DECEMFIDA, *Ham.*
Edgew. Kumaon.
St. & W. Kumaon, 7000 to 8000 ft.
A. Hushiarpur, 1500 ft.

739. SLEVOGTIA ORIENTALIS, *Griseb.*
S. verticillata, *Don.*
Edgew. Multan; Amballa.
T. T. Loodiana.
A. Hushiarpur.
Stocks. Sindh.

740. ERYTHRÆA RAMOSISSIMA, *Pers.*
T. T. Lahore; Ferozepur; Moradabad; Loodiana.
A. Jhelum; Hushiarpur.
Vicary. Amballa.
J. L. S. Peshaur.
Stocks. Beluchistan.
Griff. Afghan.

741. PLADERA PUSILLA, *Roxb.*
T. T. Rowlee Ghat; Moradabad.
A. Hushiarpur.

742. LIMNANTHEMUM CRISTATUM, *Griseb.*
Edgew. Loodiana.
T. T. Punjab; Moradabad.
J. L. S. Peshaur.

743. L. KLEINIANUM, *Griseb.*
Edgew. Multan; Gopal-mochar.
T. T. Moradabad.

HYDROPHYLLACEÆ.

744. HYDROLEA ZEYLANICA, *L.*
Nama zeylanica, *Vahl.*
Royle. Northern plains of India.
T. T. Moradabad; Punjab.
Edgew. Radaur.

EHRETIACEÆ.

745. **Ehretia aspera**, *Roxb.*
T. T. Lahore.
A. Jhelum; Hushiarpur.
J. L. S. Peshaur.

746. **E. floribunda**, *Royle.*
Edgew. Raj-ban (Kyarda-Dhun).
T. T. Meerut; Moradabad.
Stocks. Beluchistan.

747. **E. lævis**, *Roxb.*
Edgew. Seikh Protected States; Khizerabad.
T. T. Moradabad; Loodiana; Delhi.
St. & Wint. Kumaon, 1000 ft.
A. Hushiarpur, "Cheela," "Chilla."
Edgew. Seikh States, "Chamror."

748. **E. obtusifolia**, *Hochst.*
Edgew. Sha-bilawal.
Fleming. Salt range.
Stocks. Sukker; Beluchistan.

749. **E. serrata**, *Roxb.*
Edgew. Multan; Shadra valley.
T. T. Cult. Jamu.
St. & Wint. Kumaon, 1000–5000 ft.
A. Hushiarpur.

750. **E. viminea**, *Wall.*
Edgew. Kumaon; Banda.
St. & Wint. Kumaon, 2500 ft.

751. **Tournefortia subulata**, *Hochst.*
T. Edgeworthii, *DC.*
Messerschmidtia indica, *Benth.* (*Royle*).
Edgew. Multan; Loodiana.
T. T. Delhi; Ferozepur; Lahore.
Vicary. Delhi; Ferozepur; Salt range.
Stocks. Sindh.
Fleming. Salt range; Jelallpur.

752. **T. Royleana**, *DC.*
Messerschmidtia hispida, *Benth.*
Royle. Delhi.

753. **Coldenia procumbens**, *L.*
Stocks. Sindh.

754. HELIOTROPIUM CINERASCENS, *Steud.*
Stocks. Sindh, no. 630, above 4000 ft.; Beluchistan.

755. H. EUROPÆUM, *L.*
Edgew. Multan; Amballa.
T. T. Delhi; Punjab; Lahore.
A. Jhelum; Hushiarpur.
J. L. S. Peshaur.
Vicary. Googerat.
Stocks. Sindh.

756. H. LUTEUM, *Poir.*
J. L. S. Peshaur.
Griff. Afghan.
Stocks. Sindh; Beluchistan.

757. H. OPHIOGLOSSUM, *Stocks, MS.*
Stocks. Sindh.
Frere. Beluchistan. (*Hb. Stocks,* no. 466. This, in Edgeworth's list of Stocks's plants, is named *H. ditrichum,* J. E. S.)

758. H. OVALIFOLIUM, *Vahl.*
H. coromandelianum, *Retz.*
Royle. Delhi.
Stocks. Sindh.

759. HELIOTROPIUM, sp.
H. f. & T. list, Herb. No. 10.
Vicary. Sindh; Salt range.

760. HELIOTROPIUM.
H. strigosum, *Willd.*
H. brevifolium, *Wall.*
H. bicolor, *Hoch.*
Edgew. Multan.
T. T. Moradabad; Karnal to Delhi; Lahore.
A. Jhelum; Hushiarpur.
J. L. S. Peshaur.
Stocks. Beluchistan.
Frere. Beluchistan.
Fleming. Salt range.

761. H. SUPINUM, *L.*
Edgew. Punjab; Multan.
Hamilton. Patna.
Stocks. Sindh.

762. H. UNDULATUM, *Vahl.*
H. ramosissimum, *Sieb.*
Edgew. Multan; Balanwali.
T. T. Punjab.
A. Jhelum; Hushiarpur.
J. L. S. Peshaur.
Fleming. Salt range.
Stocks. Sindh.
Griff. Afghan.

CORDIACEÆ.

763. CORDIA LATIFOLIA, *Roxb.*
St. & Wint. Kumaon, 1000 feet.
A. A cultivated tree in the Punjab.

764. C. MYXA, *L.*
Edgew. Multan; Amballa, cultivated.
A. Jhelum; Hushiarpur, cultivated throughout the Punjab, and at Hushiarpur it looks indigenous, called "Chumroor" and "Lessoora."

765. C. OBLIQUA, *Willd.*
T. T. Lahore; Moradabad.

766. C. ANGUSTIFOLIA, *Roxb.*
T. T. Moradabad, hort.; Lahore.

767. GYNAION VESTITUM, *A. DC., H. f. & T.*
Edgew. Garwhal, 3000 to 4000 ft.
T. T. Garwhal.
A. Rupur; Budlee; Jhelum; Mount Tilla.
J. L. S. Mount Tilla.

BORAGINACEÆ.

768. ONOSMA ECHIOIDES, *Sm.*
Fleming. Salt range, 5000 ft.
St. & Wint. Kumaon.
T. T. Kashmir.

769. LITHOSPERMUM ARVENSE, *L.*
A. Jhelum; Hushiarpur.
Vicary. Peshaur.
Stocks. Beluchistan.
J. L. S. Peshaur.

770. SERICOSTOMA PAUCIFLORUM, *Stocks.*
Vicary. Sindh.
Stocks. Sindh.

771. ARNEBIA CORNUTA, *Fisch.*
Stocks. Beluchistan.
Griff. Afghan.

772. A. ECHIOIDES, *A. DC.*
J. L. S. Peshaur; Trans Indus.
J. Young (*hb. Edgew.*). Attock.
Fleming. Salt range.

773. A. GRIFFITHII, *Boiss.*
Fleming. Salt range.
Vicary. Peshaur.
Griff. Afghan.

774. A. HISPIDISSIMA, *DC.*
(Lithospermum vestitum, *Wall.*, according to Royle.)
Royle. Arid plains of Northern India.
Edgew. Multan.
T. T. Moradabad; Delhi; Punjab.
A. Jhelum; Hushiarpur.
Fleming. Punjab.
Stocks. Sindh.

775. NONNEA NIGRICANS, *DC.*
Stocks. Beluchistan.
Griff. Afghan.

776. N. PULLA, *DC.*
N. Edgeworthii, *DC.*
Edgew. Malwa; Punjab; Multan; Lahore.
T. T. Punjab; Ferozepur; Loodiana; Lahore.
A. Jhelum; Hushiarpur.
J. L. S. Peshaur.
Vicary. Attock.

777. LYCOPSIS ARVENSIS, *L.*
J. L. S. Peshaur.
Vicary. Peshaur.
Griff. Afghan.

778. ANCHUSA HISPIDA, *Forsk.*
Edgew. Punjab; Multan; banks of Chenab.
T. T. Punjab.
A. Jhelum.
Fleming. Salt range.
Vicary. Peshaur.
Stocks. Beluchistan.
Griff. Afghan.

779. **Bothriospermum tenellum**, *F. & M.*
Edgew. Banda.
A. Jhelum.

780. **Trichodesma Aucheri**, *Dcne.*
Vicary. Boogta Hills.
Stocks. Beluchistan.

781. **T. africanum**, *Br.*
Edgew. Multan; Punjab; Chandnot.
Vicary. Sindh.
Stocks. Sindh.

782. **T. indicum**, *Br.*
Edgew. Multan.
T. T. Punjab; Moradabad.
A. Jhelum.
J. L. S. Peshaur.
Stocks. Indus basin.
Frere. Beluchistan.
Griff. Afghan.

783. **Cynoglossum micranthum**, *Desf.*
Edgew. Amballa.
T. T. Punjab; Moradabad.
A. Jhelum.
J. L. S. Peshaur?

784. **Asperugo procumbens**, *L.*
Vicary. Peshaur.
Stocks. Beluchistan.
Griff. Afghan.

785. **Echinospermum glochidiatum**, *DC.*
Fleming. Salt range; Moch-pur (*hb. Edgew.* no. 398; *hb. Fleming,* no. 249).

786. **E. Vahlianum**, *Lehm.*
Fleming. North side of Salt range (*hb. Edgew.* no. 6155; *hb. Fleming,* No. 41.)

787. **Rochelia rectipes**, *Stocks.*
Fleming. Salt range.
Stocks. Beluch.
Griff. Afghan.

788. **R. stellulata**, *Rchb.*
Fleming. Salt range.
Vicary. Peshaur.
J. L. S. Peshaur.
Stocks. Beluchistan.
Griff. Afghan.

CONVOLVULACEÆ.

789. **Evolvulus alsinoides**, *L.*
T. T. Moradabad; Lahore.
A. Jhelum; Hushiarpur.
J. L. S. Peshaur.
Stocks. Sindh; Beluchistan.
Vicary. Sindh.

790. **Cressa cretica**, *L.*
C. indica, *Retz.*
Edgew. Multan; Punjab.
A. Jhelum.
Vicary. Sindh.
Stocks. Indus basin; Sindh.
Frere. Beluchistan.

791. **Seddera latifolia**, *Hochst.*
Stocks. Sindh; Beluchistan.
Vicary. Sindh.

792. **Porana paniculata**, *Roxb.*
T. T. Punjab; Jamu.
A. Hushiarpur, "Thourphŭllee."

793. **Convolvulus arvensis**, *L.*
Edgew. Multan.
T. T. Lahore; Punjab; Moradabad.
A. Jhelum; Umritsur; Hushiarpur.
J. L. S. Peshaur.
Stocks. Indus basin.
Frere. Beluchistan.
Griff. Afghan.

794. **C. glomeratus**, *Chois.*; *Wight, Ic.* 1366.
Fleming. Punjab.
Stocks. Sindh.
Vicary. Sindh.
Frere. Beluch.

795. **C. lanuginosus**, *Desr.*
C. capitatus, *Cav.*
C. saxatilis, *Vahl.*
A. Salt range, on limestone.
Stocks. Beluchistan.

796. C. MACROPHYLLUS, *Sieb.*
Stocks. Beluchistan ; Sindh.
Dalzel. Sindh.

797. C. PLURICAULIS, *Chois.*
Edgew. Multan ; Balanwali.
T. T. Lahore ; Moradabad ; Punjab.
A. Jhelum ; Hushiarpur.
J. L. S. Peshaur.
Vicary. Peshaur.
Griff. Afghan.

798. C. RHYNCHOSPERMUS, *Hoch.*
Stocks. Sindh.

799. CONVOLVULUS (species new).
H. f. & T. list, no. 5.
Stocks's list, no. 430 (called by Stocks *C. arvensis*, is not that plant).
Stocks. Sindh.

800. CALONYCTION MURICATUM, *Don.*
T. T. Moradabad ; Punjab.
A. Jhelum.

801. IPOMÆA CHRYSEIDES, *Bot. Regis.*
T. T. Punjab ; Moradabad.

802. I. COPTICA, *Roth.*
Royle. Delhi, arid parts.

803. I. FILICAULIS, *Blume.*
Royle. Northern India, arid parts.

804. I. PES-CAPRÆ, *L.*
Vicary. Sindh.
Stocks. Sindh.

805. I. PES-TIGRIDIS, *L.*
Edgew. Multan.
T. T. Punjab ; Moradabad ; Lahore.
Stocks. Indus basin.
Frere. Beluch.

806. I. PILOSA, *Chois.*
Royle. North-west India.
Edgew. Amballa.
T. T. Punjab.
A. Jhelum.
Stocks. Indus basin.

807. I. reptans, *Poir.*
Royle. North-west India.
T. T. Lahore; Moradabad.
Edgew. Multan.
A. Philor; Sutlej.
Stocks. Indus basin.

808. I. sessiliflora, *Roth.*
Edgew. Multan.
T. T. Punjab; Lahore.
A. Jhelum.
J. L. S. Peshaur.
Stocks. Indus basin.

809. I. Turpethum, *Br.*
T. T. Moradabad.
Edgew. Banda.

810. Quamoclit coccinea, *Moench.*
A. Cult. in gardens all over the Punjab.

811. Batatas edulis, *Chois.*
Royle. Hort. North-western India.
T. T. Cult. Lahore.
A. Very commonly cultivated by natives, and a good market article about Umritsur. "Chuk-kunder," "Sweet potato."

812. B. paniculata, *Chois.*
Royle. Arid parts of North-west India.

813. B. pentaphylla, *Chois.*
Edgew. Multan; Amballa.
T. T. Lahore; Moradabad.
A. Jhelum; Hushiarpur; Umritsur.
Stocks. Sindh.
Frere. Beluchistan.

814. Pharbitis Nil, *Chois.*
Edgew. Multan.
T. T. Moradabad; Lahore.
A. Jhelum; Hushiarpur.
J. L. S. Peshaur.
Stocks. Indus basin.

815. Rivea hypocrateriformis, *Chois.*
Edgew. Multan.
T. T. Moradabad; Lahore.
Stocks. Sindh.

816. R. ornata, *Chois.*
T. T. South of Lahore.
A. Jhelum.

817. Cuscuta europæa, *L.*
Stocks. Above 4000 ft., Beluch.

818. C. oxypetala, *Boiss.*
Stocks. Sindh; Indus basin.
Frere. Beluchistan.

819. C. planiflora, *Tenore.*
Edgew. Multan, from Yarkand seed.
Stocks. Beluchistan.
Griff. Afghan.

820. C. reflexa, *Roxb.*
Edgew. Multan.
T. T. Punjab.
A. Jhelum; Hushiarpur; Philor; Umritsur.
J. L. S. Peshaur.
A. Grows on Zizyphus, Ficus, Adhatoda, in great luxuriance at Hushiarpur, covering the "Baer" trees like seaweed.

SOLANACEÆ.

821. Nicotiana Tabacum, *L.*
A. Cultivated throughout the Punjab. "Tamak," Tobacco.

822. Datura alba, *Nees.*
T. T. Punjab; Lahore; Moradabad.
A. Jhelum (and not *D. Stramonium*, as in 'Jhelum Flora').
J. L. S. Peshaur.
Stocks. Indus basin.

823. D. fastuosa, *L.*
Edgew. Multan, cult.; Loodiana.
A. Jhelum; Hushiarpur, near houses.

824. D. Stramonium, *L.*, var. Wallichii, *Dunal.*
Edgew. Beeas valley.
T. T. Jamu, 6000 ft.; Simla, 8000 ft.
A. The Jhelum species is *D. alba*, and not this.

825. Hyoscyamus micranthus, *Ledb.*
Stocks. Sindh, from the plains, 640 feet to 4000 feet.
Griff. Afghan.

826. H. pusillus, *L.*
Fleming. Salt range.
J. L. S. Peshaur.

T. T. Ladak, 10,000 feet.
Stocks. Beluchistan.
Griff. Afghan.

827. Scopolia mutica, *Don.*
Edgew. Lahore.
T. T. Lahore.
Vicary. Sindh.

828. S. præalta, *Don.*
T. T. Nubra; Piti, 15,000 feet.
J. L. S. Peshaur.

829. Nicandra physaloides, *Gaert.*
T. T. Punjab, cult. to 7000 ft.; Simla.
A. Perfectly naturalized at all the hill stations.
A European child at Simla poisoned with the fruit of this; the seeds and portions of the leaves were found in the stomach. The symptoms a mixture of those produced by *Datura* and *Hyoscyamus*.

830. Physalis divaricata, *Don.*
Edgew. Amballa; Loodiana.

831. P. angulata, *L.*
T. T. Moradabad; *Griff.*, Afghan.

832. P. minima, *L.*
T. T. Punjab; Moradabad; Lahore.
A. Jhelum.
Stocks. Beluchistan.
Griff. Afghan.
J. L. S. Peshaur.

833. P. peruviana, *L.*
A. Commonly cultivated in the gardens of Europeans, but with difficulty ripens its fruit called "Cape-Gooseberries," "Ma-kow."

834. Capsicum frutescens, *L.*
Punjab, cultivated extensively by the natives. "Mirch," "Lal-mirch."

835. Solanum gracilipes, *Jacq.*
Edgew. Lower Punjab; Multan; Sandal Bar.
A. Jhelum.
J. L. S. Not in the valley of Peshaur.
Vicary. Boogta Hills.
Stocks. Sindh; Beluchistan.

836. S. indicum, *L.*
T. T. Simla; Moradabad.
St. & Wint. Kumaon, 5000 feet.
Stocks. Sindh.

837. S. MELONGENA, *L.*
A. Punjab, cultivated in all native gardens; called "Baingăn," "Brinjal," Eggplant.

838. S. NIGRUM, *L.*
Edgew. Multan.
T. T. Simla, 8000 feet; Lahore.
St. & W. Kumaon.
A. Jhelum; Hushiarpur, called "Ma-Kon." The ripe berries eaten by the hill people and European children without any bad effects.
J. L. S. Peshaur.
Stocks. Beluchistan.
Griff. Afghan.

839. S. SANCTUM, *L.*
S. coagulans, *Del.*
T. T. Jamu; Lahore.
St. & W. Kumaon, 1000 ft.
A. Jhelum; Hushiarpur.
Stocks. Beluchistan; Sindh.

840. S. TRILOBATUM, *L.*
Stocks. Indus basin.

841. S. TUBEROSUM, *L.*
A. Cultivated by natives, as well as Europeans, in the Punjab. "Alū," Potato. It is planted at the end of the hot weather and collected about December. If planted in January, the plant fails to produce tubers (at Umritsur), and ends in immense stems, flowers, and fruit. The incoming hot weather seems to run the plant all to leaves and seed. At from 3000 to a little above 4000 feet the plant fails to produce tubers.
Careful data regarding the limits of altitude at which good tubers are raised would be valuable, as well as under what circumstances two crops could be raised during the year in the Punjab plains.

842. S. VERBASCIFOLIUM, *L.*
Edgew. Khiserabad.
T. T. Moradabad; Karnál; Punjab.
A. Hushiarpur.

843. S. XANTHOCARPUM, *Schrd.*
S. Jacquinii, *Willd.*
Edgew. Multan.
T. T. Moradabad; Lahore; Jamu.
A. Jhelum; Hushiarpur.
J. L. S. Peshaur.

844. LYCOPERSICUM ESCULENTUM, *Sieb.*
A. Cultivated. "Love-apple," "Tomato."

845. WITHANIA COAGULANS, *Don.*
Puneeria coagulans, *Stocks.*
Edgew. Multan.
T. T. Simla Hills; Punjab.
A. Jhelum; Salt range.
Fleming. West of Indus; Salt range; Dehra-jat.
Vicary. Punjab.
J. L. S. Peshaur.
Stocks. Beluchistan; Sindh.
Griff. Afghan.

846. W. SOMNIFERA, *Don.*
Physalis somnifera, *L.*
Edgew. Multan.
T. T. Lahore; Moradabad.
A. Jhelum.
J. L. S. Peshaur.
Stocks. Sindh; Indus basin.
St. & Wint. Kumaon.

847. LYCIUM EUROPÆUM, *L.*
L. indicum, *Wight.*
L. Edgeworthii, *DC.*
Edgew. Multan; Seikh Protected States; Thanesar; Sirindh.
T. T. Lahore; Karnál; Amballa.
Vicary. Delhi to Ferozepur.
A. Umritsur.
Stocks. Sindh.
Frere. Beluca.
Edgew. Seikh States, "Kangoo."

SCROPHULARIACEÆ.

848. VERBASCUM THAPSUS, *L.*
T. T. Lahore; Moradabad; Ladak, 9000 feet.
A. Jhelum; Hushiarpur; Goodaspur; Umritsur.
J. L. S. Peshaur.
Vicary. Amballa.
Griff. Afghan.

849. V. CELSIOIDES, *Benth.*
Edgew. Thanesar (no other known locality). According to Edgeworth passes into *Celsia coromandeliana,* Vahl.

850. CELSIA COROMANDELIANA, *Vahl.*
Edgew. Multan ; Thanesar.
T. T. Moradabad ; Punjab ; Lahore.
A. Jhelum ; Hushiarpur.
J. L. S. Peshaur.
Stocks. Sindh.

851. LINARIA CABULICA, *Benth.*
Vicary. Boogta Hills.
J. L. S. Peshaur, Hazara.
Stocks. Beluchistan.
Griff. Afghan.

852. L. MINOR, *L.*
Fleming. Salt range.
Vicary. Upper Punjab.
Stewart. Hazara.

853. L. RAMOSISSIMA, *Wall.*
Edgew. Multan.
T. T. Jamu ; Kumaon.
A. Jhelum.
J. L. S. Peshaur.
Stocks. Sindh.

Var. INCANA.
J. L. S. Hazara.
Vicary. Boogta Hills.
Stocks. Beluchistan.
Griff. Afghan.

854. L. SPHÆROCARPA, *Benth.*
Antirrhinum glaucum, *Stocks, MS.*
Vicary. Hala range.
Stocks. Sindh.
Griff. Afghan.

855. L. TRIORNITHOPHORA, *Willd.*
A. Jhelum garden-weed, escape.

856. ANTIRRHINUM ORONTIUM, *L.*, var. *β*, INDICUM.
Edgew. Multan ; Amballa.
T. T. Moradabad ; Punjab.
A. Jhelum.
J. L. S. Peshaur.
Vicary. Amballa.
Griff. Afghan.
Fleming. Salt range.

857. **Scrophularia cabulica**, ***Benth.***
J. L. S. Peshaur.
Griff. Afghan.

858. **S. scabiosæfolia**, ***Benth.***
A. Jhelum.
Vicary. Peshaur.

859. **Anticharis arabica**, ***Endl.***
Fleming. Salt range.
Stocks. Sindh; Beluchistan.

860. **Doratanthera linearis**, ***Benth.***
Edgew. Multan; Ferozepur; Punjab; Sha-kote.
T. T. Ferozepur; Lahore.
Vicary. Ferozepur.
Stocks. Sindh.

861. **Mimulus gracilis**, ***Br.***
M. strictus, *Benth.*
A. Jhelum; Hushiarpur.
Edgew. Punjab; Sha-nahr; Radaur.
T. T. Punjab; Jamu, 2000 to 3000 feet; banks of Chenab.
Vicary. Punjab.
J. L. S. Peshaur.

862. **Mazus rugosus**, ***Lour.***
Edgew. Multan; Chandnot; Khiserabad.
T. T. Moradabad; Jamu; Punjab.
Lady Dalhousie. Amballa.
A. Jhelum; Hushiarpur.
J. L. S. Peshaur.
Griff. Afghan.

863. **Lindenbergia macrostachya**, ***Benth.***
Edgew. Multan; Kalesar-Dhun.
T. T. Punjab; Jamu.
A. Jhelum.
Fleming. Salt range.
Vicary. Amballa.

864. **L. polyantha**, ***Royle.***
T. T. Punjab.
A. Jhelum.
Lady Dalhousie. Agra.
Vicary. Boogta Hills.

865. L. URTICÆFOLIA, *Lehm.*
Stemodia ruderalis, *Gaert.*
Edgew. Multan; Sha-kote; Delhi.
T. T. Punjab; Jamu; Moradabad.
A. Jhelum.
Stocks. Beluchistan.

866. LIMNOPHILA GRATIOLOIDES, *Br.*
T. T. Punjab; Moradabad.
Stocks. Indus basin.

867. HERPESTIS HAMILTONIANA, *Benth.*
T. T. Moradabad; Punjab.

868. H. MONNIERIA, *H., B. & K.*
Edgew. Multan.
T. T. Lahore; Jamu; Punjab.
A. Jhelum; Hushiarpur.
J. L. S. Peshaur.
Fleming. Salt range.
Stocks. Indus basin.

869. VANDELLIA CRUSTACEA, *Benth.*
T. T. Punjab; Moradabad.

870. V. ERECTA, *Benth.*
Gratiola integrifolia, *Roxb.*
T. T. Moradabad; Punjab.

871. ILYSANTHES PARVIFLORA, *Benth.*
T. T. Moradabad; Punjab.
A. Hushiarpur.

872. BONNAYA BRACHIATA, *Link.*
Edgew. Punjab.
T. T. Moradabad; Punjab.

873. B. VERONICÆFOLIA, *Spr.*
B. verbenæfolia, *Spr.*
T. T. Punjab; Chenab; Moradabad.

874. PEPLIDIUM HUMIFUSUM, *Del.*
Stocks. Indus basin, No. 551.

875. BUDDLEIA ASIATICA, *L.*
B. Neemda, *Ham.*
Edgew. Kalesar-Dhun.
T. T. Jamu, 4000 to 6000 feet.
A. Jhelum; Hushiarpur.
J. L. S. Peshaur.
Vicary. Raulpindee.

876. B. CRISPA, *Benth.*
T. T. Jamu, 5000 to 6000 feet.
Stocks. Beluchistan.
Griff. Afghan.

877. B. MADAGASCARIENSIS, *Vahl.*
A. Hushiarpur, escape, cult. in gardens frequently.

878. VERONICA AGRESTIS, *L.*
Edgew. Punjab; Amballa.
T. T. Jamu.
A. Jhelum; Hushiarpur.
J. L. S. Peshaur.
Stocks. Beluchistan.
Griff. Afghan.

879. V. ANAGALLIS, *L.*
Edgew. Punjab; Multan.
T. T. Lahore; Punjab; Moradabad.
A. Jhelum; Hushiarpur.
Vicary. Punjab.
J. L. S. Peshaur.
Stocks. Beluch.

880. V. BUXBAUMII, *Tenore.*
Edgew. Multan.
T. T. Moradabad; Punjab.

881. V. CHAMÆDRYS, *L.*
J. L. S. Hazara.

882. STRIGA EUPHRASIOIDES, *Benth.*
Edgew. Multan.
T. T. Punjab; Moradabad.
A. Jhelum.

883. S. HIRSUTA, *Benth.*
Stocks. Sindh.

884. S. OROBANCHOIDES, *Benth.*
Royle. Seharanpur.
Stocks. Sindh; Indus basin.

885. CAMPYLANTHUS RAMOSISSIMUS, *Wight.*
Stocks. Sindh; Beluchistan.

886. LEPTORHABDOS PARVIFLORA, *Benth.*
Edgew. Himalaya, 4000 to 9000 feet.
T. T. Kumaon, 5000 to 10,000 feet.
J. L. S. Peshaur.

OROBANCHACEÆ.

887. **Phelipæa Calotropidis**, *Walp.*
Hamilton. Loodiana; Ferozepur.
Edgew. Multan, on *Calotropis.*
T. T. Punjab; Loodiana, on *Calotropis.*
Griff. Loodiana; Mysore, on *Calotropis* and *Capparis aphylla.*

888. P. **indica**, *G. Don.*
T. T. Punjab.
Lady Dalhousie. Superior Gangetic plain.
Stocks. Beluchistan.
Griff. Afghan.

889. P. **lutea**, *Desf.*
T. T. Punjab; Lahore, on *Salvadora*; Loodiana.
Stocks. Sindh.
Griff. Afghan.

890. P. **ramosa**, *C. A. M.*
T. T. Jamu, 5000 to 7000 ft.
Stocks. Beluchistan.

891. **Orobanche cernua**, *Loef.*
Stocks. Sindh; Beluchistan.
Griff. Afghan.

LENTIBULARIACEÆ.

See Oliver, L. Soc. Journal, vol. iii. 174, on Indian *Utriculariæ.*

892. **Utricularia diantha**, *Roem. et Sch.*
U. elegans, *Wall.*
U. biflora, *Roxb.*
Edgew. Loodiana.
Oliver. North-west India, *herb. Hook.*
Royle. North-west India.

893. U. **flexuosa**, *Vahl.*
U. fasciculata, *Roxb.*
Edgew. Loodiana.
Oliver. Tropical India.

894. **Utricularia** (species).
Perhaps *vulgaris*, L.
J. L. S. Peshaur.

BIGNONIACEÆ.

895. CALOSANTHES INDICA, *Blum.*
Bignonia indica, *Roxb.*
T. T. Forest-tree, Rohilkand.
A. Hushiarpur; Pathan-kote forest, frequent. "Tat-palung." The scythe-like fruit characterizes the tree.

896. MILLINGTONIA HORTENSIS, *L. fil.*
Bignonia suberosa, *Roxb.*
A. Hushiarpur; Umritsur; Lahore; Googerat. A cultivated tree, called "Akas-neem" and "Neem-jal."

897. SPATHODEA STIPULATA, *Wall.*
A. Hushiarpur, a characteristic shrub of lower hills, on sandstone, called "Summee."

898. TECOMA UNDULATA, *Don.*
T. glauca, *Decais.*
Edgew. Multan; Seikh Protected States, "Rahere," "Jogini."
A. Jhelum; Hushiarpur; Googerat.
J. L. S. Peshaur.
Fleming. Salt range.
Stocks. Beluchistan to Kurrachee; Sindh.
Griff. Punjab, "Rahere."

899. AMPHICOME EMODI, *Royle.*
A. Jhelum; Mt. Tilla; Ft. Mungla.
Parish. Punjab.
Vicary. Peshaur.
Fleming. Trans Indus; Kalabag.
Griff. Afghan.

ACANTHACEÆ.

900. THUNBERGIA FRAGRANS, *Roxb.*
A. Cult. Hushiarpur.

901. ELYTRARIA CRENATA, *Vahl.*
Royle. Jumna, arid banks.
Edgew. Punjab; Sirindh; Loodiana.
T. T. Moradabad; Punjab.

902. EBERMAIERA GLAUCA, *Nees.*
T. T. Moradabad; Superior Gangetic plain.
Vicary. Dehra-Dhun.

903. **Hygrophila polysperma**, *T. And.*
Hemiadelphis polysperma, *Nees.*
Edgew. Delhi canal; Radaur.
T. T. Moradabad; Jamu, 3000 ft.; Punjab.
A. Hushiarpur.
Stocks. Sindh; Indus basin.
Griff. Afghan.
T. Anderson. "Trop. Himalaya from Bhotan to Jamu."

904. **H. spinosa**, *T. And.*
Barleria longifolia, *L.*
Asteracantha longifolia, *Nees.*
T. T. Moradabad; Punjab.

905. **Ruellia longifolia**, *Stocks.*
Dipteracanthus longifolius, *Stocks.*
Stocks. Sindh; Beluchistan.

906. **R. patula**, *Jacq.*
Dipteracanthus patulus, *Nees.*
Edgew. Punjab; Multan; Sha-kote.
Fleming. Salt range.
Stocks. Sindh; Indus basin.

907. **R. prostrata**, *Poir.*
Dipteracanthus prostratus, *Nees.*
Royle. Seharanpur.
T. T. Moradabad; Punjab.
A. Jhelum.
T. Anderson. Ceylon to Punjab.

908. **Hemigraphis hirta**, *T. And.*
Ruellia hirta, *Vahl.*
Edgew. Amballa.
T. T. Moradabad; Loodiana.

909. **Æchmanthera Wallichii**, *Nees.*
Edgew. Multan.
T. T. Garwhal, trop.
Lady Dalhousie. Simla.
St. & Wint. Kumaon, 3000 ft.
A. Hushiarpur.

910. **Dædalacanthus nervosus**, *T. And.*
Justicia nervosa, *Vahl.*
Eranthemum Edgeworthianum, *Nees.*
Royle. North-west Himalaya.
Vicary. Dehra-Dhun.
Edgew. Bural-Bar (in the hills).

T. T. Simla, 1000 to 2000 feet.
A. Hushiarpur.

911. BARLERIA ACANTHOIDES, *Vahl.*
Stocks. Sindh.

912. B. CRISTATA, *L.*
B. ciliata, *Roxb.*
Edgew. Multan; Sirindh; Rhol.
T. T. Punjab; Lahore; Jamu; Moradabad.
A. Jhelum; Hushiarpur.
J. L. S. Peshaur.

913. B. HOCHSTETTERI, *Nees.*
Stocks. Sindh.

914. B. PRIONITIS, *Linn.*
B. hystrix, *Linn.*
B. trispinosa, *Vahl.*
Royle. Seharanpur.
T. T. Moradabad; Jamu.
Stocks. Sindh; Indus basin.

915. LEPIDAGATHIS CALYCINA, *Hochst.*
Stocks. Sindh.
Dalzel. Sindh.

916. L. CRISTATA, *Willd.*
Royle. Jumna; North-west India.
Stocks. Sindh; Deesa.

917. L. HYALINA, *Nees.*
L. riparia, *Nees.*
T. T. Jamu, 2000 to 3000 feet.
A. Hushiarpur.

918. L. PURPURICAULIS, *Nees.*
St. & Wint. Kumaon.
A. Hushiarpur.

919. BLEPHARIS BOERHAAVIÆFOLIA, *Pers.*
Acanthus madraspatensis, *L.*
Royle. Seharanpur; Jumna.
T. T. Moradabad; Superior Gangetic plain.

920. B. EDULIS, *Pers.*
Acanthodium spicatum, *Delil.*
Acanthus edulis, *Vahl.*
Edgew. Multan; Punjab; Sandal Bar.
Stocks. Sindh; Beluchistan.
Griff. Afghan.

921. B. MOLLUGINIFOLIA, *Pers.*
B. madraspatana, *L.*
T. T. Moradabad; Superior Gangetic plain.
Royle. Jumna; Delhi.

922. B. SINDICA, *Stocks, MS.*
Vicary. Ferozepur.
Stocks. Sindh.

923. ANDROGRAPHIS ECHIOIDES, *Nees.*
Royle. Superior Gangetic plain.
Edgew. Sewaliks.
T. T. Punjab; Jamu.
T. Anderson. In Punjab and Superior Gangetic plain.
Vicary. Saugur.

924. JUSTICIA ADHATODA, *L.*
Adhatoda Vasica, *Nees.*
T. T. Moradabad; Punjab; Jamu; not Lahore.
A. Jhelum; Hushiarpur.
J. L. S. Peshaur.
T. Anderson. Subtropical Himalaya, even to Peshaur; throughout the plains of India.
A. Hushiarpur, "Bunsootee."

925. J. HETEROCARPA, *T. And.*
Stocks. Sindh.
Vicary. Ferozepur.

926. J. PEPLOIDES, *T. And.*
Rostellaria peploides, *Nees.*
T. T. Punjab; Moradabad.
A. Jhelum.

927. RUNGIA PECTINATA, *Nees.*
R. parviflora, *Nees.*
T. T. Punjab; Meerut; Moradabad.
A. Hushiarpur.

928. R. REPENS, *Nees.*
Justicia repens, *L.*
Edgew. Sirhind.
T. T. Moradabad.
Stocks. Indus basin.

929. DICLIPTERA ROXBURGHII, *Nees.*
D. bupleuroides, *Nees.*
Royle. Plains, north-west India.
T. T. Punjab; Moradabad.

A. Jhelum; Hushiarpur.
J. L. S. Peshaur.
Fleming. Salt range.
Griff. Afghan.

930. PERISTROPHE BICALYCULATA, *Nees.*
Edgew. Multan.
T. T. Punjab.
Stocks. Indus basin; Sindh.

PEDALIACEÆ.

931. SESAMUM INDICUM, *L*
S. orientale, *L.*
A. Cultivated very largely throughout the Punjab for its seed, from which oil is extracted. The plant, "Tilee," yields a bland oil, "Til ka thail," "Meta-thail," used largely for culinary purposes.
T. T., Edgew., A., J. L. S.

LABIATÆ.

932. OCIMUM BASILICUM, *L.*
Edgew. Multan, cult.; Amballa.
T. T. Delhi; Loodiana; Moradabad.
A. Jhelum, cult.; Hushiarpur, cult., but also indigenous on low hills.

933. O. MENTHÆFOLIUM, *Hochst.*
Stocks. Sindh.

934. O. SANCTUM, *L.*
Edgew. Multan, cult.
T. T. Moradabad; Lahore, cult.; doubt if ever indigenous.
A. Jhelum, low ranges of hills.

935. ORTHOSIPHON PALLIDUS, *Royle.*
Royle. Jumna.
Edgew. Punjab; Loodiana.
Stocks. Beluchistan.

936. O. VIRGATUS, *Wall.*
Edgew. Sub-Sewalik jungle.
T. T. Jamu, 2000 ft.; Kumaon.
Jacq. Mohun pass.
St. & Wint. Kumaon, 3000 feet.

937. Plectranthus rugosus, *Benth.*
Edgew. Kumaon.
T. T. Jamu; Chamba: Kumaon.
A. Jhelum; Hushiarpur.
J. L. S. Peshaur.

938. Anisochilus carnosum, *Wall.*
Wall. Sup. Gangetic plain.
Royle. Jumna plain.
Edgew. Banda.

939. Pogostemon plectranthoides, *Desf.*
T. T. Kumaon.
St. & Wint. Kumaon, 800 feet.
A. Hushiarpur; Naree.

940. Dysophylla verticillata, *Benth.*
T. T. Jamu.

941. Colebrookia oppositifolia, *Sm.*
Edgew. Sewaliks; Kalesar.
T. T. Jamu.
A. Jhelum; Mt. Tilla; Hushiarpur.
Fleming. Salt range.
J. L. S. Peshaur.

942. Mentha incana, *Willd.*, var. Royleana.
Edgew. Cult. Multan.
T. T. Simla hills, 2000 feet.
J. L. S. Peshaur.
Griff. Afghan.

943. M. sylvestris, *L.*
Royle. North-west India.
T. T. Punjab plains.

944. M. viridis, *L.*
A. Cult. Punjab. "Podeena," Mint.

945. Lycopus europæus, *L.*
T. T. Punjab plains, 1000 ft.
J. L. S. Peshaur.

946. Salvia ægyptiaca, *L.*
Vicary. Peshaur; Boogta Hills.
Stocks. Beluchistan alone, 4000 feet.

947. S. GLUTINOSA, *L.*
S. hians, *Royle.*
T. T. Jamu, 6000 feet; Simla.
J. L. S. Peshaur.

948. S. LANATA, *Roxb.*
T. T. Simla, 7000 feet.
Lady Dalhousie. Simla.
St. & Wint. Kumaon, 5500 feet.
J. L. S. Peshaur.

949. S. MOORCROFTIANA, *Wall.*
T. T. Kashmir, 7000 ft.; Simla, 6000 ft.
A. Jhelum; Salt range, 2000 feet.
J. L. S. Peshaur.

950. S. PLEBEIA, *Br.*
Royle. Plains of India.
Edgew. Multan; Khizerabad.
T. T. Punjab; Jamu; Chamba; Lahore.
A. Jhelum; Hushiarpur.
J. L. S. Peshaur.
Stocks. Indus basin.
Griff. Afghan.

951. S. PUMILA, *Benth.*
Royle. Probably *S. acaulis,* Vahl, hb. Royle, as Falconer has specimens from Delhi also.
Edgew. Punjab; Delhi; Multan.
J. Young. Attock (*hb. Edgew.*).
Fleming. Salt range.
A. Jhelum.
J. L. S. Peshaur.
Vicary. Boogta Hills.
Stocks. Sindh; Beluchistan, above 4000 feet.
Griff. Afghan.

952. ORIGANUM NORMALE, *DC.*
T. T. Jamu.
Fleming. Salt range.

953. THYMUS SERPYLLUM, *L.*
A. Fort Mungla; Jhelum (not in 'Flora of Jhelum').
T. T. Jamu, 9000 feet.

954. MICROMERIA BIFLORA, *Benth.*
T. T. Punjab; Jamu.

A. Jhelum; Hushiarpur.
J. L. S. Peshaur.
Vicary. Punjab.

955. SCUTELLARIA REPENS, *Ham.*
T. T. Simla, 1000 to 6000 feet; Kumaon.
St. & Wint. Kumaon, 2000 to 5000 feet.
A. Hushiarpur.

956. NEPETA GRACILIFLORA, *Benth.*
T. T. Punjab; Jamu, 1500 feet.
Jacq. Punjab.
St. & Wint. Garwhal, 1000 feet.

957. N. RUDERALIS, *Ham.*
N. calaminthoides, *Benth.*
Royle. Punjab.
Edgew. Himalaya, 3000 ft.; Khizerabad.
T. T. Jamu, 3000 feet.
A. Jhelum.
Griff. Afghan.

958. LALLEMANTIA ROYLEANA, *Benth.*
Dracocephalum Royleanum, *Wall.*
Edgew. Multan, cult.; Lahore.
T. T. Cult. Lahore.
A. Jhelum; Rhotas, not from cultivation.
Fleming. Salt range.
J. L. S. Peshaur.
Stocks. Beluchistan.
Griff. Afghan.

959. LAMIUM AMPLEXICAULE, *L.*
T. T. Kumaon, 9000 feet.
A. Jhelum.
J. L. S. Peshaur.
Griff. Afghan.

960. ANISOMELES OVATA, *Br.*
Edgew. Amballa.
T. T. Punjab; Moradabad; Lahore.
A. Jhelum.
J. L. S. Peshaur.

961. STACHYS PARVIFLORA, *Benth.*
A. Jhelum.
Vicary. Peshaur.
Griff. Afghan.

962. OTOSTEGIA AUCHERI, *Stocks.*
Stocks. Beluchistan.

963. O. LIMBATA, *Benth.*
Ballota limbata, *Benth.*
J. Young, hb. Edgew. Attock.
Jacq. Pind-Dadun-Khan.
Fleming. Salt range.
A. Jhelum, low hills.
J. L. S. Peshaur.
Vicary. Punjab.

964. LEUCAS ASPERA, *Spr.*
L. nutans, *Spr.*
Edgew. Punjab.
T. T. Punjab; Superior Gangetic plain.
A. Jhelum.
Stocks. Sindh.

965. L. CEPHALOTES, *Spr.*
T. T. Punjab; Superior Gangetic plain.
A. Jhelum; Hushiarpur.
Jacq. Rajaori.
J. L. S. Peshaur.
Griff. Afghan.

966. L. LANATA, *Benth.*
T. T. Jamu, 4000 feet; Rampur, 3300 feet.
Jacq. Rajaori.

967. L. URTICÆFOLIA, *Benth.*
Edgew. Multan; Bar; Thanesar.
T. T. Loodiana, between Meerut and Delhi.
A. Jhelum.
Vicary. Punjab.
Stocks. Sindh.

968. LEONOTIS NEPETÆFOLIA, *Br.*
Royle. Banks of Jumna.
T. T. Moradabad.
St. & W. Kumaon, 2000 ft.

969. EREMOSTACHYS LACINIATA, *Bunge.*
J. L. S. Peshaur.
Griff. Afghan.
Stocks. Beluchistan.

970. E. SUPERBA, *Royle.*
Royle. Dehra-Dhun.
Vicary. Peshaur.

971. E. Vicaryi, *Benth.*
A. Jhelum; Salt range.
Vicary. Peshaur.
Stocks. Beluchistan, 3000 feet.

972. Holmskioldia sanguinea, *Retz.*
St. & Wint. Kumaon, 2500 ft.; Hushiarpur, cult., and a weed in gardens.

973. Ajuga bracteosa, *Wall.*
A. remota, *Benth.*
A. parviflora, *Benth.*
Edgew. Amb. (Hushiarpur district).
T. T. Kumaon, 4000 to 8000 feet.
A. Hushiarpur, common weed.
J. L. S. Peshaur.

VERBENACEÆ.

974. Lippia nodiflora, *Rich.*
H. f. & T. Everywhere in India, but not Afghan or Thibet.
T. T. Punjab; Lahore.
A. Jhelum; Hushiarpur.
Edgew. Multan.
J. L. S. Peshaur.
Stocks. Indus basin.

975. Verbena officinalis, *L.*
Edgew. Multan; Amballa.
T. T. Punjab; Lahore.
A. Jhelum; Hushiarpur.
Fleming. Punjab.
J. L. S. Peshaur.
Stocks. Beluchistan.
Griff. Afghan.

976. Bouchea marrubifolia, *Wt.*
Vicary. Sindh.
Stocks. Sindh.

977. Priva leptostachya, *Juss.*
Stocks. Beluchistan, under 4000 feet.

978. Caryopteris Wallichiana, *Schau.*
Edgew. Kalesar-Dhun; San-Sadhaura.
T. T. Jamu; Kumaon.

St. & W. Kumaon, 1000 ft.
A. Hushiarpur, "Bunkar."
Fleming. Salt range.

979. LANTANA ALBA, *Mill.*
L. indica, *Roxb.*
Edgew. Thanesar.
A. Jhelum; Hushiarpur.
J. L. S. Peshaur.
Stocks. Beluchistan.

980. L. DUBIA, *Wall.*
Royle. Jumna river.
T. T. Moradabad.

981. VITEX NEGUNDO, *L.*
T. T. Jamu, 3000 feet; Lahore.
A. Jhelum; Hushiarpur, "Bunna."
J. L. S. Peshaur.
Stocks. Beluchistan.

Var. BICOLOR, *Willd.*
Edgew. Multan; Amballa.

982. PREMNA MUCRONATA, *Roxb.*
Edgew. North-west India.
T. T. Kumaon.

983. TECTONIA GRANDIS, *L. fil.*
A. Cultivated, Hushiarpur, and grows well, ripening its seed. "Teak."

984. GMELINA ARBOREA, *Roxb.*
Edgew. Sadhaura; Thanesar.
T. T. Kumaon.
St. & Wint. Kumaon, 1500 feet.
A. Hushiarpur forests and hills; at Goodaspur cantonments cultivated largely. At Hushiarpur called "Komara."
Edgew. Sadhaura, "Kumhar."

985. CLERODENDRON FRAGRANS, *Willd.*
A. Cult., and thought much of by the natives.
Is it an escape at Hushiarpur?

986. C. PHLOMOIDES, *L.*
Edgew. Multan; Thanesar; Bud-bud.
T. T. From Lahore to Moradabad, but not common.
A. Jhelum.
Stocks. Sindh, cult.

987. C. SERRATUM, *Spr.*
T. T. Kumaon; Simla.
St. & W. Kumaon, 4000 feet.

988. C. SIPHONANTHUS, *Br.*
T. T. Moradabad.
A. Hushiarpur, cult.

989. DURANTA PLUMIERI, *L.*
A. Frequently cult. in gardens; a fine shrub.

990. CALLICARPA MACROPHYLLA, *Vahl.*
T. T. Punjab; Jamu Hills; Moradabad.
"Flax made from this," *H. f. & T.*

PLANTAGINACEÆ.

991. PLANTAGO CILIATA, *Desf.*
A. Jhelum.
Fleming. Salt range; Mt. Tilla.
Vicary. Peshaur.
Stocks. Beluchistan.

992. P. DECUMBENS, *Forsk.*
P. Ispaghula, *Roxb.*
P. eriantha, *Decais.*
Edgew. Multan, cult.; Radaur; Amballa.
T. T. Punjab.
Jacq. Punjab.
A. Jhelum.
J. L. S. Peshaur.
Vicary. Punjab.
Stocks. Beluchistan.

993. P. ARENARIA, *W. & K.*
P. indica, *hb. Royle.*
Royle. North-west India.
J. L. S. Peshaur.
Griff. Afghan.

994. P. AMPLEXICAULIS, *Cav.*
P. Bauphula, *Edgew.*
Edgew. Multan; Sirhind; Sangrūr.
T. T. Lahore.
Jacq. Punjab.
A. Jhelum.

J. L. S. Peshaur.
Vicary. Punjab; Sindh.
Stocks. Beluchistan.
Griff. Afghan.

995. P. LANCEOLATA, *L.*
J. L. S. Peshaur.
Vicary. Peshaur.
Stocks. Beluchistan.
Griff. Afghan.

996. P. MAJOR, *L.*
T. T. Kumaon, 5000 to 11,000 feet.
J. L. S. Peshaur.
Stocks. Beluchistan, above 4000 feet.
Griff. Afghan.

997. P. STOCKSII, *Boiss.*
Stocks. Sindh, No. 594.

MONOCHLAMYDEÆ.

PARONYCHIACEÆ.

998. HERNIARIA HIRSUTA, *L.*
Edgew. herb. Jhelum.
A. Jhelum; Fort Mungla.
T. T. East of Ferozepur.
J. L. S. Peshaur.
Jacq. Punjab.
Stocks. Beluchistan.
Griff. Afghan.

999. GYMNOCARPUS FRUTICOSUS, *Forsk.*
Stocks. Sindh.

1000. COMETES APICULATA, *Delile.*
Vicary. Boogta Hills.
Stocks. Sindh.

NYCTAGINACEÆ.

1001. BŒRHAAVIA DIFFUSA, *L.*
B. procumbens, *Roxb.*
Edgew. Multan; Amballa.

T. T. Moradabad; Lahore.
A. Jhelum; Kaunpur.
J. L. S. Peshaur.
Stocks. Indus basin; Sindh; Beluchistan.

1002. B. ELEGANS, *Choisy.*
B. esculenta, *Edgew.*
Edgew. Multan; Rechnab-Bar.
Stocks. Sindh; Beluchistan.

1003. B. REPANDA, *Willd.*
B. dichotoma, *Vahl.*
T. T. Moradabad; Seharanpur; Punjab.
A. Jhelum; Mt. Tilla.
Stocks. Indus basin.

1004. B. REPENS, L.
B. vulvariæfolia, *Poir.*
Edgew. Multan-Bar; Rechnab-Bar.

1005. B. VERTICILLATA, *Poir.*
Stocks. Sindh.

1006. MIRABILIS JALAPA, *L.*
A. Spread from cultivation, an extensive weed in some favourable localities, both yellow- and pink-flowered varieties. Kalka to Simla; Hushiarpur; Pathan-Kote to Dalhousie; Tropical valleys.

POLYGONACEÆ.

1007. PTEROPYRUM AUCHERI, *Jb. et Sp.*
Stocks. Sindh.

1008. POLYGONUM AVICULARE, *L.*
T. T. Lahore.
A. Jhelum; Hushiarpur, "Kara-bara."
J. L. S. Peshaur.

1009. P. BARBATUM, *L.*
T. T. Moradabad; Lahore.
A. Jhelum.
J. L. S. Peshaur.

1010. P. CONVOLVULUS, *L.*
Royle. North-west India.

1011. P. FLACCIDUM, *Roxb.*
P. tenellum, *Roxb.*
T. T. Moradabad; Ravee Doab.
J. L. S. Peshaur.

1012. P. GLABRUM, *Willd.*
Royle. Seharanpur.
Edgew. Multan; Loodiana.
T. T. Loodiana; Moradabad; Lahore.
Stocks. Sindh.
Griff. Afghan.

1013. P. LAPATHIFOLIUM, *L.*
P. simlense, *hb. Royle.*
Royle. Simla.
T. T. West of Lahore; Loodiana; Banks of Chenab.
J. L. S. Peshaur.

1014. P. NUMMULARIFOLIUM, *Meis.*
Edgew. Rūpur.

1015. P. PERSICARIA, *L.*
T. T. Punjab.
A. Jhelum.
J. L. S. Peshaur.

1016. P. PLEBEIUM, *Br.*
P. herniarioides, *Del.*
P. Dryandri, *Spr.*
P. Roxburghii, *Meisn.*
Royle. Plains of India.
Edgew. Multan; Madhapur; Sirindh; Balanwali.
T. T. Punjab; Kumaon; Moradabad.
St. & W. Kumaon, 1000 feet.

1017. P. SALICORNIOIDES, *Jb. et Sp.*
Vicary. Sindh.

1018. P. SERRULATUM, *Lag.*
T. T. Punjab; Moradabad.

1019. CALLIGONUM POLYGONOIDES, *L.*
Edgew. Sandal Bar; Adun-wan; Multan; Punjab.
Vicary. Peshaur.
Stocks. Sindh.

1020. RUMEX ACETOSA, *L.*
Edgew. Badhri-nath.
T. T. Kumaon.
A. Jhelum (?).

1021. R. HASTATUS, *Don.*
T. T. Kumaon.
St. & Wint. Kumaon, 1000–6000 feet.
J. L. S. Peshaur.

1022. R. VESICARIUS, *L.*
A. Jhelum; Salt range.
J. L. S. Peshaur.
Vicary. Peshaur.
Stocks. Beluchistan.
A. Indigenous to the above localities, but is also cultivated in the Punjab as a pot-herb, and generally so thoughout India.

1023. R. WALLICHII, *Meisn.*
R. dentatus, *L.*
R. conglomeratus, *Murr.*
R. acutus, *Roxb.*
Edgew. Multan; Khizerabad.
T. T. Punjab; Moradabad; Lahore.
A. Hushiarpur; Jhelum.
J. L. S. Peshaur.
Stocks. Sindh.

1024. ATRAPHAXIS (near LANCEOLATA).
T. T. Jugduluk Pass.
Vicary. Sindh.
Frere. Beluchistan.

CHENOPODIACEÆ.

1025. ATRIPLEX GRIFFITHII, *Moq.*
Stocks. Sindh.
Griff. Afghan; Kurrachee.

1026. A. LACINIATUM, *L.*
T. T. Lahore; Punjab; Thibet to 15,000 feet.
A. Jhelum; Doomun.
J. L. S. Peshaur.

1027. A. REPENS, *Roth.*
Vicary. Sindh.

1028. SPINACIA OLERACEA, *L.*
Edgew. Cult. Multan; Jhung.
T. T. Cult. Lahore.
Edgew. "Cultivated throughout the Punjab."
A. "Spinach," "Pālŭk."

1029. **Beta vulgaris**, *L.*
B. orientalis, *Heyne.*
B. bengalensis, *Roxb.*
H. f. & T. Cultivated throughout India.
Royle. "Paluk," cultivated.
Edgew. Multan; Amballa, cultivated.
J. L. S. Peshaur.
A. The leaves used as a pot-herb, "Paluk." The root-stock "Chookunder," "Beet-root."

1030. **Kochia arenaria**, *Roth.*
Edgew. Multan; Amballa.
Stocks. Sindh.

1031. **K. scoparia**, *Schrd.*
Royle. North-west India.
T. T. Punjab.
Jacq. Punjab.
Griff. Googeranwalla; Jellalabad.

1032. **Chenopodium album**, *L.*
Edgew. Amballa.
T. T. Punjab; Moradabad; Lahore.
A. Jhelum.
J. L. S. Peshaur.
Royle. "Bhutwa."

1033. **C. Botrys**, *L.*
T. T. 10,000 feet, Simla; Kumaon; Garwhal.
J. L. S. Peshaur.

1034. **C. hybridum**, *L.*
T. T. Kunaur, high altitudes.
J. L. S. Peshaur.

1035. **C. murale**, *L.*
C. Hookerianum, *Moq.*
Edgew. Multan.
T. T. Loodiana; Chenab; Punjab, everywhere.
A. Jhelum.

1036. **Suæda indica**, *Moq.*
S. fruticosa, *L.*
Salsola Lana, *Edgew.*
Edgew. Multan; Amballa.
T. T. Lahore; Ferozepur; Punjab.
A. Jhelum.

Fleming. Salt range.
J. L. S. Peshaur.
Vicary. Delhi.
Stocks. Sindh; Indus basin.
Griff. Afghan.

1037. S. MONOICA, *Forsk.*
Vicary. Sindh.

1038. SALSOLA KALI, *L.*
S. Jacquemontii, *Moq.*
T. T. Tibet, 15,000 feet.
J. L. S. Peshaur.
Stocks. Beluchistan.
Griff. Afghan.

1039. CAROXYLON FŒTIDUM, *Moq.*
Salsola indica, *hb. Royle.*
Royle. Delhi.
Edgew. Multan; Thanesar; Bar.
T. T. Punjab.
Vicary. Punjab.
A. Jhelum.
J. L. S. Peshaur.
Stocks. Sindh.
Frere. Beluchistan.

1040. C. GRIFFITHII, *Moq.*
T. T. Punjab.
Edgew. Punjab; Multan.
J. L. S. Peshaur.
Stocks. Beluchistan.
Frere. Beluchistan.
Griff. Afghan.

1041. C. SALICORNICUM, *Moq.*
Anabasis salicornia.
Edgew. Punjab; Bar,
Fleming. Salt range.
Griff. Afghan.

1042. ANABASIS MULTIFLORA, *Moq.*
Haloxylon multiflora, *Bunge.*
Edgew. Multan.
A. Jhelum.
J. L. S. Peshaur.
Griff. Afghan.

1043. ANABASIS, species, near A. FLORIDA, *Bunge.*
Vicary. Indus; Punjab.

BASELLACEÆ.

1044. **Basella rubra,** ***L.***
B. alba, ***L.***
T. T. **Cultivated in India instead of Spinach.**

AMARANTACEÆ.

1045. **Alternanthera sessilis,** ***Br.***
A. denticulata, ***Br.***
Edgew. **Multan.**
T. T. **Moradabad ; Punjab ; Lahore.**
A. **Jhelum.**
J. L. S. **Peshaur.**
Stocks. **Indus basin.**
Griff. **Afghan.**

1046. **Achyranthes aspera,** ***L.***
Royle. **North-west India.**
Edgew. **Multan.**
T. T. **Moradabad ; Punjab ; Lahore.**
A. **Jhelum ; Hushiarpur.**
J. L. S. **Peshaur.**
Stocks. **Indus basin.**
Frere. **Beluchistan.**

1047. **Ærua Bovii,** ***Edgew.***
Edgew. **Multan.**
Griff. **Afghan.**

1048. **Æ. brachiata,** ***Mart.***
Edgew. **Multan ; Jhung ; Bar.**
T. T. **Moradabad ; Punjab.**
Stocks. **Sindh.**

1049. **Æ. javanica,** ***Juss.***
Edgew. **Sandal Bar ; Multan ; Loodiana.**
T. T. **Punjab ; Lahore ; Sutlej ; Delhi.**
A. **Jhelum ; Hushiarpur.**
J. L. S. **Peshaur.**
Royle. **Arid banks of Jumna.**

1050. Æ. SCANDENS, *Wall.*
Royle. Suen range; Giree River.
Edgew. Multan.
T. T. Punjab; Moradabad.
A. Jhelum.

1051. Æ. LANATA, *Juss.*
Royle. North-west India.
T. T. Patna to Monghir.
Stocks. Indus basin.

1052. DIGERA ARVENSIS, *Forsk.*
Desmochæta muricata, *W. Ic.*
Achyranthes alternifolia, *L.*
Royle. Jumna, arid banks.
Edgew. Multan.
T. T. Moradabad; Lahore; Punjab.
A. Jhelum.
J. L. S. Peshaur.
Stocks. Sindh.

1053. EUXOLUS VIRIDIS, *L.*
E. viridis, var. caudatus, *Moq.*
Edgew. Multan.
T. T. Moradabad; Punjab.
A. Jhelum; Umritsur; Philor.

1054. MENGEA TENUIFOLIA, *Moq.*
Amaranthus tenuifolius, *Willd.*
A. angustifolius, *Roxb.*
Edgew. Multan.
A. Jhelum.
Stocks. Sindh; Indus basin.
T. T. Moradabad.

1055. PUPALIA LAPPACEA, *Moq.*
Desmochæta lappacea, *Moq.*
Edgew. Multan; Amballa.
T. T. Punjab; Delhi; Moradabad.
A. Jhelum; Hushiarpur.
J. L. S. Peshaur.

1056. AMARANTHUS BLITUM, *L.*
Edgew. Multan; Amballa.
T. T. Punjab.

Var. POLYGONOIDES.
Euxolus polygamus, *Moq.*
Amaranthus polygamus, *L.*
Royle. Cultivated in India.
T. T. Moradabad; Punjab; Lahore.
J. L. S. Peshaur.

1057. A. FRUMENTACEUS, *Roxb.*
A. speciosus, *Bot. Mag.* 2227.
H. f. Catalogue. Cult. everywhere in India; Simla to Sikkim.
Royle. Cultiv. Mysore.

1058. A. GANGETICUS, *L.*
A. Mangostanus, *L. fil.*
A. oleraceus, *Wt. Ic.*
Royle. Cultivated.
Edgew. Multan, cult.
T. T. Punjab; Lahore, "occasionally as a weed, perhaps not indigenous."

1059. A. RETROFLEXUS, *L.*
T. T. Moradabad; Lahore.

1060. A. CAUDATUS, *L.*
T. T. Cult. Lahore.
Griff. Afghan.
Stocks. Beluchistan.

1061. CELOSIA ARGENTEA, *L.*
Edgew. Multan.
T. T. Lahore.
A. Jhelum; Hushiarpur.
J. L. S. Peshaur.
Stocks. Indus basin.

1062. DEERINGIA CELOSIOIDES, *Br.*
Royle. Foot of the Himalaya.
T. T. Jamu; Punjab.
A. Hushiarpur.

THYMELACEÆ.

1063. DAPHNE OLEOIDES, *L.*
Stocks. Sindh (hills?).
Griff. Afghan.

1064. THYMELÆA ARVENSIS, *Lam.*
J. Young, hb. Edgew. Attock.
T. T. Plains below Jamu; Upper Punjab.
Griff. Afghan.

1065. DIARTHRON VESICULOSUM, *C. A. M.*
Vicary. Peshaur.
Griff. Afghan.

LAURACEÆ.

1066. TETRANTHERA ROXBURGHII, *Nees.*
Royle. North-west India.
T. T. Garwhal, 3000 feet.
St. & Wint. Kumaon, 3500 feet.
A. Jhelum; Mt. Tilla, indigenous; Poonch valley.
Royle. Wood called "Mueda-lukree."

ARISTOLOCHIACEÆ.

1067. ARISTOLOCHIA BRACTEATA, *Retz.*
Edgew. Banda.
Stocks. Sindh.

PIPERACEÆ.

1068. CHAVICA ROXBURGHII, *Miq.*
Piper longum, *Roxb.*
A. Cultivated at Hushiarpur, and apparently succeeds well. This is its most northern cultivation in India. "Mug," "Peepra-a-mur."

EUPHORBIACEÆ.

1069. EUPHORBIA THYMIFOLIA, *Burm., Lam.*
Edgew. Amballa.
T. T. Moradabad.
A. Jhelum.
J. L. S. Peshaur.
Frere. Beluch.

1070. E. CHAMÆSYCE, *Willd.*
Edgew. Multan; Amballa.
A. Jhelum; Hushiarpur.

1071. E. DRACUNCULOIDES, *Lam.*
T. T. Moradabad; Punjab; Lahore.
A. Jhelum.
J. L. S. Peshaur.

1072. E. GRANULATA, *Forsk.*
E. villosa, *Hb. Royle.*
Edgew. Multan; Balanwali.
T. T. Punjab.
Vicary. Sindh.
Stocks. Sindh (*hb. Edgew.*).

1073. E. HELIOSCOPIA, *L.*
Edgew. Multan; Loodiana; Jhung.
T. T. Punjab; Lahore.
A. Jhelum.
J. L. S. Peshaur.
Stocks. Beluchistan.
Griff. Afghan.

1074. E. HYPERICIFOLIA (of Indians), not of *L.* (*Hook. fil.*).
E. indica, *Lam.*
E. cassioides, *Presl.*
E. parviflora, *Roxb.*
Edgew. Amballa.
T. T. Punjab; Lahore.
A. Jhelum.
J. L. S. Peshaur.
Frere. Beluch.
Griff. Afghan.

1075. E. NEPALENSIS, *Boiss.*
Edgew. Loodiana; Khizerabad.
A. Jhelum.

1076. E. NERIIFOLIA, *Willd.*
Stocks. Beluchistan.

1077. E. PEPLUS, *L.*
J. L. S. Peshaur?

1078. E. PILULIFERA, *L.*
T. T. Moradabad; Simla.

1079. E. ROSEA, *Retz.*
T. T. Amballa.

1080. E. ROYLEANA, *Bois.*
E. pentagona, *Ham.*
T. T. Valleys leading into the hills, Kalka to Simla.
A. Hushiarpur hills, profuse, utilized for hedges, called "Thor." Sutlej valley profuse; not Mt. Tilla or the Salt range, not near Fort Mungla or Poonch.

1081. E. sanguinea, *Hochst.*
T. T. Punjab; Lahore.

1082. E. Tirucalli, *Willd.*
A. Hushiarpur, cultivated in hedges, rare; not met with anywhere else in the Punjab. Kurrachee, common.

1083. Stillingia sebifera, *Michx.*
A. Introduced by Europeans, grows well, produces ripe seed from which many of the Punjab trees have already been raised, as at Hushiarpur &c.

1084. Tragia cannabina, *L. fil.*
Royle. Jumna.

1085. Acalypha ciliata, *Forsk.*
T. T. Jamu.
St. & Wint. Simla, 4000 ft.

1086. A. indica, *L.*
Royle. Jumna.

1087. Jatropha curcas, *L.*
Royle. Near Hurdwar, called "Bagh-Burinda."
A. Hushiarpur, a common road-side shrub, on the Purwain range. A frequent garden-shrub in Punjab, and, as at Umritsur, becomes a weed; introduced.

1088. Ricinus communis, *L.*
Edgew. Multan, cult.; Kalesar-Dhun, indigenous.
T. T. Lahore; Moradabad.
A. Jhelum; Hushiarpur.
J. L. S. Peshaur.
Stocks. Beluch. to Kurrachee.
A. A common weed-shrub near dwellings throughout the less arid parts of the Punjab, on low hills, not so much near dwellings. Castor-oil, "Arund," "Arind."

1089. Mallotus philippinensis, *Müll.*
Rottlera tinctoria, *Roxb.*
T. T. Forests at foot of hills.
A. Jhelum; Hushiarpur.
Stocks. Sindh.

1090. Baliospermum polyandrum, *Wight.*
B. indicum, *Decais.*
Croton polyandrum, *Roxb.*
Royle. Jumna.
T. T. Near the hills.
A. Jhelum.
J. L. S. Peshaur.

1091. CROZOPHORA PLICATA, *Juss.*
C. Rottleri, *Juss.*
Royle. Jumna.
Edgew. Multan; Amballa.
T. T. Ferozepur; Lahore.
Stocks. Sindh; Indus basin.

1092. C. TINCTORIA, *Juss.*
C. oblongifolia, *Juss.*
Edgew. Amballa; Multan.
T. T. Punjab; Lahore; Ferozepur.
A. Jhelum; Hushiarpur.
J. L. S. Peshaur.
Stocks. Sindh.

1093. BRIDELIA MONTANA, *Willd.*
St. & Wint. Kumaon, 3000 feet.
A. Hushiarpur.

1094. ANDRACHNE ASPERA, *Spr.*
J. L. S. Peshaur.
Stocks. Sindh.

1095. A. TELEPHIOIDES, *L.*
A. Jhelum.
Fleming. Salt range.
J. L. S. Peshaur.
Stocks. Beluchistan.

1096. PHYLLANTHUS URINARIA, *L.*
T. T. Banks of Chenab.

1097. P. NIRURI, *L.*
Edgew. Multan.
T. T. Moradabad; Lahore.
A. Jhelum; Mt. Tilla.
Frere. Beluchistan.

1098. P. MADRASPATENSIS, *L.*
Edgew. Banda.
Stocks. Indus basin.

1099. P. EMBLICA, *L.*
Emblica officinalis, *Gært.*
T. T. Moradabad; Jamu; Punjab, near the hills.
Edgew. Multan (cult.).
A. Jhelum cult., not Mt. Tilla or the Salt range. Hushiarpur hills and plains, indigenous, "Howla," "Aowla." A religious prejudice of the Hindoos against cutting the trees; the fruit is preserved and eaten.

1100. P. RETICULATUS, *Müller*.
P. multiflorus, *Willd*.
P. pentandra, *Hb. Royle*.
Anisonema multiflora, *Wight*.
Royle. North-west India.
T. T. Meerut; Moradabad.
Stocks. Sindh; Indus basin.

1101. BRADLEIA BIFARIA, *Roxb*.
Glochidion tomentosum, *Dalz*.
G. bifarium, *Forsk*.
St. & Wint. Kumaon, 4000–5000 feet.
A. Hushiarpur.

1102. BISCHOFFIA JAVANICA, *Blum*.
Andrachne trifoliata, *Roxb*.
Royle. Jumna.
Edgew. Sewaliks.

1103. FLUGGEA VIROSA, *Roxb*.
Edgew. Radaur.
J. L. S. None near Peshaur; frequent beyond the Indus to the south of Peshaur.
Stocks. Sindh.

1104. F. RETUSA, *Roxb*.
Royle. Jumna.
T. T. Moradabad; Chenab valley.

1105. BUXUS SEMPERVIRENS, *L*.
Fleming. Salt range.
A. Salt range, called "Pupper." The branches, with the leaves on, used for thatching. Boxwood.

1106. PUTRANJIVA ROXBURGHII, *Wall*.
Edgew. Amballa, cult.
T. T. Moradabad, cult.
St. & Wint. Kumaon, 1000 feet.
Edgew. Native name "Jiapota."

CERATOPHYLLACEÆ.

1107. CERATOPHYLLUM DEMERSUM, *L*.
T. T. Moradabad.
J. L. S. Peshaur.
Griff. Afghan.

URTICACEÆ.

1108. POUZOLZIA PENTANDRA, *Br.*
Urtica pentandra, *Roxb.*
T. T. Moradabad; Seharanpur; Jamu; west of Chenab; Punjab.
Griff. Afghan.

1109. URTICA DIOICA, *L.*
T. T. Thibet.
Fleming. Salt range.

1110. DEBREGEASIA HYPOLEUCA, *Wedd.*
Missiessya hypoleuca, *Wedd.*
Urtica bicolor, *Roxb.*
T. T. Jamu.
Jacq. Base of the Himalaya.
J. L. S. Peshaur.

1111. BŒHMERIA PLATYPHYLLA, *Don.*
A. Hushiarpur; Purwain range of hills.
Fleming. (A species) at Kutha, Salt range, *hb. Edgew.* no. 8115 (*hb. Fleming,* no. 85).

1112. FORSKOLEA TENACISSIMA, *L.*
A. Jhelum, Mt. Tilla, and Salt range.
J. Young, hb. Edgew. Attock.
J. L. S. Peshaur.
Stocks. Sindh (hills?).

1113. PLECOSPERMUM SPINOSUM, *Trécul.*
St. & Wint. Kumaon, 1000 feet.

ARTOCARPACEÆ.

1114. ARTOCARPUS INTEGRIFOLIA, *L. fil.*
Edgew. Jagadhri garden.
A. Jackfruit, called "Kuthul" and "Burhul;" cultivated at Amb and Hushiarpur, bearing fine large fruit.

1115. A. LAKOOCHA, *Roxb.*
St. & Wint. Kumaon forests, indigenous, up to 3000 feet.
A. Cultivated, Hushiarpur gardens, called "Dahoo."

1116. **Streblus asper**, *Lour.*
Trophis aspera, *Willd.*
T. T. Moradabad.
St. & Wint. Kumaon, 1000 feet.
Royle. (Species) Arid banks of Jumna.

MORACEÆ.

1117. **Ficus cunia**, *Ham.*
Ficus conglomerata, *Roxb.*
T. T. Kumaon.
St. & W. Kumaon, 4000 feet.
A. Hushiarpur; Purwain range of hills.

1118. **F. glomerata**, *Roxb.*
A. Pind-Dadun-Khan, a cultivated tree; Hushiarpur, a lofty forest-tree, "Gular."

1119. **F. oppositifolia**, *Willd.*
T. T. Jamu; Kumaon, 1000 ft.

1120. **F. macrophylla**, *Miq.*
J. L. S. Peshaur.

1121. **F. cordifolia**, *Roxb.*
St. & Wint. Kumaon, 1500 ft.
A. Hushiarpur, "Budha," "Pilkun." Its furthest north-west range.

1122. **F. infectoria**, *Willd.*
St. & Wint. Kumaon.
A. Jhelum; Mt. Tilla.
J. L. S. Peshaur.

1123. **F. religiosa**, *L.*
Edgew. Multan; Seikh States; Loodiana.
T. T. Moradabad; Lahore.
A. Jhelum; Hushiarpur; throughout the Punjab; Sindh.
Stocks. Beluchistan; Sindh.
Edgew. Seikh States, "Peepul."
A. "Pipul."

1124. **F. carica**, *L.*
T. T. Jamu.
Fleming. Marri.
A. The Fig is cultivated all over the Punjab, rarely with good fruit, or of any size.

1125. **F. CARICOIDES**, ***Roxb.***
F. virgata, *Roxb.*
Edgew. Multan.
T. T. Moradabad; Lahore.
A. Jhelum; Hushiarpur.
J. L. S. Peshaur.
Stocks. Sindh; Beluchistan.
Griff. Afghan.

1126. **F. BENGALENSIS**, ***L.***
F. indica, *L.*
Edgew. Multan.
A. Jhelum; Hushiarpur. The largest tree I have seen of this, in the Punjab, is six miles from Hushiarpur, north-east, and covers 100 yards square of ground. The parent tree is now nearly altogether separated from its surrounding progeny. Common in the Punjab, but rare as we go northwards towards Raulpindee and Peshaur.
"Bore," "Burgot," the "Banyan" tree of Southern India.

1127. **MORUS TATARICA**, ***Desf.***
Edgew. Multan, cult.
T. T. Lahore.

1128. **M. ALBA**, ***Willd.***
M. atropurpurea, *Roxb.*
Fleming. Marri.
Stocks. Beluchistan.
T. T. Cult.
A. All the Mulberries are cultivated in the Punjab proper; none indigenous. In some localities, as at Amb, with moisture and good soil, they form splendid trees; but, as a rule, they are miserable gnarled shrubs rather than trees. "Toot."

1129. **M. INDICA**, ***Willd.***
Edgew. Multan; Amballa, cult.; Khizerabad, indigenous.
T. T. Punjab.
St. & Wint. Kumaon.

1130. **M. LÆVIGATA**, ***Wall.***
St. & Wint. Kumaon, large tree.
A. Jhelum and Hushiarpur, cult.
J. L. S. Peshaur, cult.

CANNABINACEÆ.

1131. **Cannabis sativa**, *L.*
Edgew. Multan.
T. T. Moradabad ; Simla ; Lahore.
A. Jhelum ; Hushiarpur.
J. L. S. Peshaur.

ULMACEÆ.

1132. **Celtis caucasica**, *Willd.*
St. & W. Kumaon, 2000 feet.
Fleming. Salt range.
T. T. Cult. Kashmir.
A. Jhelum.
Stocks. Sindh, cultivated.

1133. **C. australis**, *L.*
T. T. Sutlej valley, 5000 to 6000 feet, large tree.
A. Hushiarpur hills.
Griff. Afghan.

1134. **Sponia politoria**, *Planch.*
T. T. Jamu ; Kalka.
St. & W. Bhaber, Kumaon, 1000 feet.
A. Hushiarpur forest.

1135. **Ulmus campestris**, *L.*
T. T. Jamu.

PLATANACEÆ.

1136. **Platanus orientalis**, *L.*
P. vulgaris, *Spach.*
T. T. Cultivated, Lahore.
A. Cult. Umritsur ; Amb, Hushiarpur district, very fine lofty trees.
J. L. S. Peshaur, cult.
A. "Chunar," Plane tree.

AMENTACEÆ.

1137. ALNUS NITIDA, *Endl.*
J. L. S. Peshaur, at the exit of the Swat river into the plains; and banks of the Ravee in the plains.

1138. QUERCUS ILEX, *L.*
J. L. S. Peshaur. This Oak is the wood used for firewood at Peshaur, from the Khyber Pass.

1139. JUGLANS REGIA, *L.*
T. T. Jamu.
A. Hushiarpur, cultivated in the Amb garden, Hushiarpur; produces fruit at 1200 feet, "Akrot," Walnut: cult. at Raulpindee; Mt. Tilla.
J. L. S. Peshaur, cult.

1140. ENGELHARDTIA COLEBROOKIANA, *Lind.*
T. T. Nynee-tal.
St. & W. Kumaon, 4500 feet.
A. Hushiarpur forest, 1200 feet.

1141. SALIX OCTANDRA, *Del.*
Vicary. Delhi, cult.
Stocks. Sindh.
Griff. Afghan.

1142. S. BABYLONICA, *L.*
Edgew. Multan, cult.; Amballa.
T. T. Cultivated in the plains.
A. Jhelum; Hushiarpur, cultivated, "Mujnor," "Banih." In one locality near Hushiarpur, certainly not from cultivation, but apparently indigenous.
J. L. S. Peshaur?

1143. S. CAPREA, *L.*
T. T. Cultivated at Lahore to yield "Bed-mushk."
Edgew. Loodiana, cult., "Bed-i-mushk."
J. L. S. Peshaur, cultivated to yield "Bed-mushk."

1144. S. TETRASPERMA, *Roxb.*
Edgew. Punjab; Multan, cult.
T. T. Jamu hills; Lahore; banks of the Chenab in the plains of the Punjab.

1145. Populus alba, *L.*
Fleming. Marri Hills, indigenous.
J. L. S. Peshaur, cultivated.
Stocks. Beluchistan, cult.

1146. P. euphratica, *Dne.*
Edgew. Multan.
T. T. Thibet, 10,000 feet.
A. Cultivated at Jhelum, Googerat, Lahore, Philor; Indus river, immense jungles. Sindhee "Bhan," "Bahn."
Vicary. Boogta Hills.
Stocks. Sindh; Indus banks.
Griff. Banks of Sutlej, at Kyrpur, called "Sofaida;" further down the river, "Bān."
A. There seems to be a belt of river-country where this plant does not exist; I never saw it (indigenous) from Pind-Dadun-Khan to Fort Kungla, on the Jhelum, nor yet near Googerat, nor Philor, although growing well (introduced) in gardens and on road-sides, especially at Googerat. It is not in the Hushiarpur district. It reappears in the higher altitudes to 11,000 feet in Western Thibet (*T. T.*). It should do well in England.

1147. P. nigra, *L.*
P. dilatata, *Ait.*
P. fastigiata, *Desf.*
T. T. Cultivated, Lahore.
A. Cult. Jhelum, Hushiarpur, Umritsur, and throughout the Punjab.
J. L. S. Peshaur.
A. Native name "Sofaida."

CASUARINEÆ.

1148. Casuarina muricata, *Roxb.*
A. Immense trees at Amballa, cultivated round the cantonments; several species are being introduced into the Punjab. The "Beefwood" of Australia.

PINACEÆ.

1149. Pinus longifolia, *Lamb.*
T. T. Jamu.
A. Hushiarpur. The lowest elevation that this tree has as yet been found to grow, indigenous, is 1300 feet in the Geree jungle, Hushiar-

pur, where the trees are as lofty, and produce as good timber as any I have seen in the higher altitudes. Introduced, Mt. Tilla, Jhelum; cultivated from Raulpindee to Calcutta.

J. L. S. Peshaur.

A. Native name "Cheer," "Cheel." The long-leafed Pine of the Himalaya.

1150. Thuja orientalis, *L.*

A. Cultivated, Hushiarpur.

Stocks. Cult. Beluch.

A. Native name "Mahjoo." The (Chinese) Arbor vitæ.

1151. Cupressus sempervirens, *L.*

A. Cultivated in every native garden in the Punjab, "Suroo," Cypress.

J. L. S. Peshaur, cult.

Griff. Afghan.

GNETACEÆ.

1152. Ephedra ciliata, *F. & M.*

E. Alte, *C. A. M.*

Fleming. Salt range.

Vicary. Mar-gulla Pass.

Stocks. Sindh.

Dalzell. Sindh.

Griff. Afghan.

1153. E. alata, *Decaisne.*

Edgew. Multan.

Griff. Afghan.

MONOCOTYLEDONÆ.

PALMACEÆ.

1154. Chamærops Ritchiana, *Griff.*

A. Jhelum, very rare and accidental specimens; between Tullagung and Mt. Sikesar in quantity (seen quantities of leaves collected from there).

J. L. S. Peshaur; Attok.

Fleming. Mt. Sikesar and Salt range.

Stocks. Sindh; Beluchistan.

A. Jhelum, the imported leaves, called "Puttha," largely used for matting, made by people from Peshaur, at Lahore, and lately Umritsur; it is superior matting to that made from the *Phœnix*, also for ropes, &c. &c.

1155. PHŒNIX SYLVESTRIS, *Roxb.*

T. T. Lahore; Sealkote.

A. Jhelum; Mt. Tilla; Hushiarpur; Gūgrate.

Stocks. Indus basin.

A. The wild Palm, called by Hindostanees "Tarree-Kujoor." About Hushiarpur the trees have been regularly tapped for their juice, which, fermented, yields "Taree," "Toddy."

1156. P. DACTYLIFERA, *L.*

Edgew. Multan, introduced by the Arabs.

A. Jhelum, Pind-Dadun-Khan, Lahore, Umritsar, and Hushiarpur (lately).

J. L. S. Peshaur.

A. The Date-palm, "Kujoor," good fruit at Pind-Dadun-Khan, Multan. Immense groves of trees at Sukker and Kotree, Sindh.

ARACEÆ.

1157. COLOCASIA ANTIQUORUM, *Schot.*

Arum Colocasia, *Willd.*

Royle. Cultivated, North-west India, "Kuchoo," "Gaglee."

A. Punjab, cultivated.

J. L. S. Peshaur, cult.

1158. TYPHONIUM (species).

A. Jhelum; Mt. Tilla.

1159. AMORPHOPHALLUS CAMPANULATUS, *Blum.*

A. Yields a large root-stock, the size of a Swedish turnip, but flatter, called "Zumeen-Kund," is said to grow in the low hills, Hushiarpur; it is eaten to some extent by the Hindu population.

LEMNACEÆ.

1160. LEMNA POLYRHIZA, *L.*

L. orbiculata, *Roxb.*

T. T. Lahore; Kumaon, 4000 feet.

Stocks. Indus basin.

A. A species of *Lemna*, perhaps this, and *not Pistia*, as given in As. Soc. Journal, vegetation of Jhelum district.

1161. L. MINOR, *L.*
T. T. Moradabad; Iskardo.
J. L. S. Peshaur.

1162. L. TRISULCA, *L.*
J. L. S. Peshaur?

TYPHACEÆ.

1163. TYPHA ANGUSTIFOLIA, *L.*, var. ELEPHANTINA, *Roxb.*
Royle. Northern India, leaves used for matting, "Reree;" var. *elephantina*, "Putera."
T. T. Moradabad; Rechnab Doab; Lahore; Upper Punjab.
A. Sindh, "Pun," used for matting; the soft downy seeds for pillows. Hushiarpur (a species).
Stocks. Sindh. The pollen made into bread, and to be had at one season of the year only.
J. L. S. Peshaur, seeds mixed into mortar to cause it to grip, leaves used for thatch.

1164. T. LATIFOLIA, *L.*
Edgew. Multan.
J. L. S. Peshaur.
A. I have not seen specimens from either of these localities.

1165. T. MINOR, *Sm.*
Stocks. Beluchistan.
Griff. Afghan.

1166. SPARGANIUM RAMOSUM, *Huds.*
Edgew. Sha-Nahr; Buhria.
T. T. Loodiana.
Griff. Afghan.

NAIADACEÆ.

1167. NAIAS MINOR, *DC.*
Caulinia indica, *Willd.*
T. T. Moradabad.
Stocks. Indus basin.

1168. ZANNICHELLIA PALUSTRIS, *L.*
T. T. Punjab.
J. L. S. Peshaur.
Stocks. Sindh.
Griff. Afghan.

JUNCAGINACEÆ.

1169. **Ruppia maritima**, *L.*
Stocks. Sindh (Kurrachee ?)

1170. **Potamogeton rufescens**, *Schrad.*
T. T. Loodiana.
Griff. Afghan.

1171. **P. pectinatus**, *L.*
T. T. Moradabad; Lahore.
J. L. S. Peshaur (*gramineus*, L. ?, may be this plant).
Stocks. Sindh.
Griff. Afghan.

1172. **P. crispus**, *L.*
P. tuberosus, *Roxb.*
Edgew. Loodiana.
T. T. Lahore; Moradabad.
A. Jhelum; Hushiarpur.
J. L. S. Peshaur.
A. Used in the refining of sugar at Hushiarpur.

1173. **P. perfoliatus**, *L.*
Edgew. Jhung.
J. L. S. Peshaur.
Stocks. Sindh.

1174. **P. natans**, *L.*
P. indicum, *Wall.*
Edgew. Loodiana.
T. T. Moradabad; Jamu; Punjab.
Jacq. Punjab.
A. Jhelum (not in the 'Flora of Jhelum'); Hushiarpur; Philor.
J. L. S. Peshaur.
Stocks. Sindh.

1175. **Aponogeton undulatus**, *Roxb.*
Onvirandra undulata, *Edgew.*
T. T. Moradabad.

BUTOMACEÆ.

1176. **Butomus umbellatus**, *L.*
Edgew. Loodiana; Karnál.
T. T. Jalinder; Loodiana; Rechnab Doab.
J. L. S. Peshaur.

1177. **B. lanceolatus**, *Roxb.*
T. T. Moradabad.

ALISMACEÆ.

1178. **Alisma reniforme**, *Don.*
Edgew. Loodiana.
J. L. S. Peshaur.
St. & Wint. Kumaon.

1179. **A. Plantago**, *L.*
T. T. Chenab.
A. Jhelum; Hushiarpur.
J. L. S. Peshaur.
Fleming. Marri.

1180. **Sagittaria sagittifolia**, *L.*
T. T. Punjab; Loodiana; Lahore; Moradabad.
J. L. S. Peshaur.

1181. **S. cordifolia**, *Roxb.*
Edgew. Amballa.
T. T. Moradabad.
A. Jhelum; Hushiarpur.

HYDROCHARIDEÆ.

1182. **Hydrilla dentata**, *Scop.*
Serpicula verticillata, *Roxb.*
T. T. Moradabad; Lahore.
J. L. S. Peshaur.
Stocks. Sindh.

1183. **Vallisneria spiralis**, *L.*
Edgew. Loodiana.
T. T. Moradabad; Loodiana; Lahore.
A. (*Henderson*). Salt range.
J. L. S. Peshaur.
Stocks. Sindh.

ORCHIDACEÆ.

1184. **Epipactis veratrifolia**, *Boiss.*
St. & Wint. Kumaon, 7000 ft.
Vicary. Peshaur.
Griff. Afghan.

1185. **Spiranthes australis**, *L.*
Vicary. Peshaur.
Fleming. Marri.

1186. **Zeuxine sulcata**, *Lind.*
Edgew. Multan.
T. T. Punjab; Delhi to Lahore.
A. Jhelum; Hushiarpur.
J. L. S. Peshaur.
Stocks. Sindh; Indus basin.
Griff. Afghan.

1187. **Z. membranacea**, *Wight.*
Z. bracteata, *Wight. Ic.*
Stocks. Sindh.

ZINGIBERACEÆ.

1188. **Costus speciosus**, *Sm.*
T. T. Moradabad.

MUSACEÆ.

1189. **Musa sapientum**, *L.*
A. Throughout the Punjab only cultivated; in Khasia (*H. f. & T.*), 2000 to 6500 ft., indigenous.
The fruit (Plantain, "Kela") in the Punjab poor, and requires artificial heat to bring it to maturity, except, perhaps, near Delhi.

PONTEDERACEÆ.

1190. **Monochoria hastifolia**, *Presl.*
T. T. Moradabad.

1191. **M. vaginalis**, *Presl.*
T. T. Lahore; Moradabad.

COMMELYNACEÆ.

1192. **Commelyna striata**, *Hochst.*
Stocks. Sindh; Beluchistan.
Frere. Beluchistan.

1193. **C. bengalensis**, *L.*
Edgew. Amballa.
T. T. Lahore; Moradabad.
A. Jhelum; Hushiarpur.

1194. **C. communis**, *L.*
Edgew. Amballa.
T. T. Moradabad; Kunawar; Lahore.
A. Jhelum; Hushiarpur.
J. L. S. Peshaur.

IRIDACEÆ.

1195. **Iris**, sp.
J. L. S. Peshaur.

AMARYLLIDACEÆ.

1196. **Narcissus Tazetta**, *L.*
Hermione Tazetta, *Haw.*
T. T. Lahore, cultivated.
Griff. Afghan.

1197. **Narcissus**, species.
A. Cultivated.

1198. **Crinum**, species.
A. Cultivated.

1199. **Agave**, sp.

1200. **Fourcroya**, sp.
A species of each of these genera is commonly cultivated in gardens in the Punjab.

DIOSCOREACEÆ.

1201. **Discorea**, species.
Specimens too young for identification.
A. Hushiarpur. Yields a large tuber, much sought for at certain Hindu feasts. The ground where this grows is one mass of pits from the continuous digging for the tubers, called "Thurree."

1202. **D. sagittata**, *Royle.*
Royle. North-west India.

T. T. Rampur; Sutlej.
St. & W. Kumaon.
Edgew. Kumaon, 2400 feet.

1203. D. BULBIFERA, *L.*
T. T. Moradabad; Simla.
Lady Dalhousie. Simla.

LILIACEÆ.

1204. TULIPA MONTANA, *Lind.*
Jacq. No. 652.
Fleming. Salt range.
Stocks. Beluchistan.

1205. T. STELLATA, *Hook.*
Edgew. Amb, Hushiarpur.
A. Jhelum (not in the 'Flora of Jhelum'); Hushiarpur.
J. L. S. Peshaur.

1206. GAGEA BULBIFERA, *Sch.*
A. Hushiarpur.

1207. G. RETICULATA, *R. & T., Sch.*
Edgew. Amb, Hushiarpur; Sal forest, Dehra-Dhun.
Jacq. Rajaori.
Vicary. Mar-gulla Hills.
Fleming. Salt range.
Stocks. Beluchistan.
Griff. Afghan.
A. Hushiarpur (and a species at Jhelum, perhaps this).

1208. GLORIOSA SUPERBA, *L.*
T. T. Moradabad; Dehra-Dhun.

1209. ALOE, sp.
An Aloe is indigenous or apparently naturalized in the low hills of Hushiarpur; it is also cultivated, like *Sempervirens tectorum* throughout Britain, its leaves being put to much the same uses.

1210. ALLIUM CEPA, *L.* (Onion.)
Edgew. Multan, cult.
T. T. Lahore, cult.
Stocks. Beluchistan, indigenous.

1211. A. RUBELLUM, *Bieb.*
T. T. Banahal (not Punjab).

Jacq. Rajaori.
A. Jhelum; Salt range.
J. L. S. Peshaur.

1212. ALLIUM, species.
No. 26, *H.f.* list.
Vicary. Mani-Kiala.
Fleming. Salt range.

1213. SCILLA HOHENACKERI, *F. & M.*
Vicary. Mar-gulla Pass.
Griff. Afghan.

1214. SCILLA, species.
A. Jhelum.

1215. UROPETALUM HYSUDRICUM, *Edgew.*
Perhaps *U. serotinum,* Ker.
Edgew. Loodiana; Punjab.

1216. ASPHODELUS FISTULOSUS, *L.*
A. clavatus, *Roxb.*
Edgew. Multan.
T. T. Punjab; Lahore.
A. Jhelum; Hushiarpur.
J. L. S. Peshaur.
Stocks. Sindh.

1217. ASPARAGUS ASCENDENS, *Roxb.*
Edgew. Low hills; Sadhaura.
T. T. Jamu; Moradabad; Rampur.
Fleming. Salt range.
Griff. Afghan.

1218. A. CURILLUS, *Roxb.*
A. Jhelum.

1219. A. OFFICINALIS, *L.*
T. T. Moradabad, cult.
A. Cultivated, Punjab. In the gardens of Europeans only.

1220. A. MARITIMUS, *Pall.*
Stocks. Sindh.

1221. A. RACEMOSUS, *Roxb.*
Edgew. Sadhaura, lower hills.
T. T. Rowlee-Ghat; Bengal.
A. Jhelum, "Eilora."
J. L. S. Peshaur.

1222. **Asparagus**, species.
Near *officinalis*, shorter-leaved.
No. 4. *H. f. & T. catalogue.*
T. T. Lahore; Kumaon.
Vicary. Rhotas.
A. Jhelum.

1223. A. **verticillatus**, *L.*
Stocks. Beluchistan.

MELANTHACEÆ.

1224. **Bulbocodium**, new species.
A. Jhelum.
Vicary. Mar-gulla Pass.

JUNCACEÆ.

1225. **Juncus articulatus**, *L.*
J. lamprocarpus, *Erhr.*
Fleming. Marri.
J. L. S. Peshaur.
Griff. Afghan.

1226. J. **bufonius**, *L.*
Royle. Delhi.
T. T. Moradabad; Delhi; Loodiana; Lahore; Ferozepur.
A. Jhelum.
J. L. S. Peshaur.

1227. J. **dichotomus**, *Willd.*
Edgew. Thanesar.

1228. J. **uliginosus**, *Roth.*
T. T. Lahore.
Griff. Afghan.

ERIOCAULACEÆ.

1229. **Eriocaulon trilobum**, *Ham.*
Stocks. Sindh.

1230. E. **sexangulare**, *L.*
T. T. Moradabad; Seharanpur; Kumaon.

CYPERACEÆ.

1231. **Carex nubigena**, *Prescott.*
Jacq. Rajaori.

1232. C. **Wallichiana**, *Prescott.*
T. T. Moradabad; Loodiana; Jalinder; east of Ferozepur.
J. L. S. Peshaur.

1233. **Fimbristylis comata**, *Nees.*
T. T. Moradabad.

1334. F. **communis**, *Rth.*
Edgew. Multan.
T. T. Punjab; Lahore.

1235. F. **dichotoma**, *Vahl.*
T. T. Moradabad.
J. L. S. Peshaur.
Griff. Afghan.

1236. F. **diphylla**, *Vahl.*
F. ovalis, *Nees.*
T. T. Punjab; Moradabad.
J. L. S. Peshaur.

1237. F. **pallescens**, *Nees.*
T. T. Punjab.
Stocks. Sindh.
Griff. Afghan.

1238. F. **schœnoides**, *Vahl.*
T. T. Punjab.

1239. **Isolepis barbata**, *Br.*
T. T. Moradabad; Punjab; Simla.
A. Jhelum.

1240. I. **lupulina**, *Nees.*
T. T. Ferozepur to Lahore, near Chenab, Upper Punjab.
Griff. Peshaur.

1241. I. **Roylei**, *Nees.*
T. T. Punjab.

1242. I. **setacea**, *R. Br.*
T. T. Banks of Chenab.

1243. I. SUPINA, *Br.*
T. T. Moradabad; Punjab; Kumaon.

1244. I. SQUARROSA, *Vahl.*
T. T. Punjab; Chenab River.

1245. TRICHELOSTYLIS JUNCIFORMIS, *Nees.*
T. T. Punjab; Moradabad.
Jacq. Punjab.

1246. T. MILIACEA, *Nees.*
T. T. Moradabad; Punjab; Lahore.

1247. T. QUINQUE-ANGULARIS, *Nees.*
T. T. Banks of Chenab; Upper Punjab.

1248. TRICHELOSTYLIS, species.
No. 16, *H. fil. & T. T. herb. Ind. or.*
T. T. Punjab.

1249. T. TENELLA, *Nees.*
T. T. Lahore; Moradabad.
Jacq. No. 459.

1250. ABILGARDTIA MONOSTACHYA, *Vahl.*
T. T. Punjab.

1251. SCIRPUS AFFINIS, *Roth.*
Edgew. Multan.
T. T. Meerut; Punjab; Lahore.

1252. S. GROSSUS, *L. fil.*
Hymenochæte grossa, *Nees.*
Edgew. Multan.

1253. S. MARITIMUS, *L.*
T. T. Punjab; Moradabad; Lahore.
A. Jhelum.
J. L. S. Peshaur.
Stocks. Beluchistan.
Griff. Afghan.

1254. S. MUCRONATUS, *L.*
T. T. Punjab; Moradabad.

1255. MALACOCHÆTE PECTINATA, *Nees.*
T. T. Moradabad; Loodiana.
J. L. S. Peshaur.
Griff. Afghan.

1256. **Eleocharis compacta**, *Br.*
T. T. Punjab.
Griff. Afghan.

1257. **E. ovata**, *Br.*
T. T. Punjab.
Jacq. Sutlej river.

1258. **E. palustris**, *Br.*
Edgew. Multan.
T. T. Moradabad; Punjab; Lahore.
A. Jhelum.
J. L. S. Peshaur.

1259. **Eleogenus atropurpureus**, *Kunth.*
Eleocharis atropurpurea, *Kunth.*
T. T. Moradabad.

1260. **E. capitatus**, *Nees.*
Stocks. Sindh.

1261. **Limnochloa acutangula**, *Nees.*
T. T. Moradabad.

1262. **L. plantaginea**, *Nees.*
T. T. Moradabad.

1263. **Eriophorum comosum**, *Wall.*
Royle. Northern India.
T. T. Jamu.
A. Jhelum; Hushiarpur.
J. L. S. Peshaur.
Royle. North India, "Bhabbur."
A. Hushiarpur, "Buggur."

1264. **Cyperus alopecuroides**, *Roth.*
T. T. Punjab; Moradabad.
Stocks. Sindh.

1265. **C. arenarius**, *Retz.*
Stocks. Sindh.

1266. **C. aristatus**, *Roth.*
T. T. Moradabad.
Jacq. Punjab.

1267. **C. aurantiacus**, *H. & K.*
T. T. Moradabad.

1268. **C. auricomus**, *Sieb.*
T. T. Moradabad; Punjab.
(Dried roots highly odoriferous.)

1269. C. compressus, *L.*
T. T. Moradabad; Punjab.

1270. C. difformis, *L.*
T. T. Punjab; Moradabad; Lahore.
J. L. S. Peshaur.
Griff. Afghan.

1271. C. distans, *L.*
T. T. Moradabad.

1272. C. exaltatus, *Retz.*
T. T. Moradabad; Lahore.
J. L. S. Peshaur.

1273. C. flavescens, *L.*
C. capillaris, *Koen.*
T. T. Moradabad; Punjab; Iskardo.
J. L. S. Peshaur.
Stocks. Sindh.
Griff. Afghan.

1274. C. Haspan, *L.*
Edgew. Multan.
T. T. Moradabad; Punjab.
A. Jhelum.
J. L. S. Peshaur.

1275. C. infra-apicalis, *Nees.*
T. T. Moradabad; Punjab.
Griff. Afghan.

276. C. Iria, *L.*
C. pauciflorus, *Vahl.*
Edgew. Multan.
T. T. Lahore; Moradabad.

1277. C. Monti, *L. fil.*
T. T. Punjab, west of Chenab river.
Griff. Afghan.

1278. C. mucronatus, *L.*
T. T. Meerut; Moradabad.
Jacq. Punjab.
A. Jhelum.
J. L. S. Peshaur.
Griff. Afghan.
Stocks. Sindh (var. *junciformis*).

1279. C. niveus, *Retz.*
T. T. Moradabad; Punjab.

Jacq. Punjab.
A. Jhelum; Hushiarpur.
J. L. S. Peshaur.
Stocks. Sindh; Beluchistan.

1280. C. PROCERULUS, *Nees.*
Edgew. Multan.

1281. C. PULVINATUS, *N. & M.*
C. punctatus, *Rich.*
T. T. Punjab; Moradabad.

1282. C. PYGMÆUS, *Vahl.*
Isolepis Micheliana, *R. & S.*
Dichostylis Micheliana, *Nees.*
Scirpus Michelianus, *L.*
Royle. North-west India; Delhi.
Edgew. Multan.
T. T. Punjab; Moradabad; Chenab.
Jacq. Calcutta to Delhi.

1283. C. ROTUNDUS, *L.*
Edgew. Multan.
T. T. Moradabad; Meerut; Punjab; Lahore.
A. Jhelum.
J. L. S. Peshaur.
Stocks. Sindh.
Frere. Beluchistan.

1284. C. SANGUINOLENTUS, *Vahl.*
T. T. Punjab; Chenab.
Jacq. Rajaori.

1285. CYPERUS, species.
No. 32, *Hook. fil. & T. T. herb. Ind. or.*
T. T. Punjab.

1286. KYLLINGIA BREVIFOLIA, *Rottb.*
T. T. Moradabad.

1287. K. MONOCEPHALA, *L.*
T. T. Punjab.

1288. MARISCUS DILUTUS, *Nees.*
T. T. Punjab; Moradabad.

1289. M. UMBELLATUS, *L.*
T. T. Moradabad.

GRAMINEÆ.

ORYZEÆ.

1290. LEERSIA CILIATA, *Roxb.*
T. T. Moradabad.

1291. ORYZA SATIVA, *L.*
Edgew. Multan; Seikh Protected States, cultivated.
T. T. Moradabad, wild state, perhaps escaped. Cultivated throughout the Punjab, but dependent on irrigation.
A. Jhelum district, rarely cultivated; Hushiarpur, more commonly. "Dhan," "Moonjee," Rice.
J. L. S. Peshaur.

1292. HYGRORYZA ARISTATA, *Nees.*
Leersia aristata, *Roxb.*
Royle. North-west India.
T. T. Morabadad.

PHALAREÆ.

1293. ZEA MAYS, *L.*
A. Maize, Indian-corn, "Makhee," cultivated generally throughout the Punjab, as a garden product; in the lower hills more extensively.
Edgew. Multan; Seikh Protected States.
T. T. Punjab.
A. Jhelum; Hushiarpur.
J. L. S. Peshaur.

1294. COIX GIGANTEA, *Roxb.*
T. T. Upper Gangetic plain.

1295. C. LACHRYMA, *L.*
T. T. Near the hills (No. 1447).

1296. CHIONANCHE BARBATA, *Br.*
Coix barbata, *Roxb.*
T. T. Rechnab Doab; Punjab; Moradabad.
Jacq. No. 105; *Voyage,* No. 1295?

1297. CRYPSIS ACULEATA, *Ait.*
T. T. Punjab; Ferozepore.

1298. ALOPECURUS GENICULATUS, *L.*
T. T. Moradabad; Punjab.
J. L. S. Peshaur.

1299. A. PRATENSIS, *L.*
Jacq. Kashmir.
J. L. S. Peshaur.
Stocks. Beluchistan.
Griff. Afghan.

1300. PHLEUM ARENARIUM, *L.*
Jacq. Punjab.

1301. P. ASPERUM, *L.*
Jacq. Punjab.

1302. PHALARIS MINOR, *Retz.*
Edgew. Multan.
T. T. Lahore ; Ferozepur ; Moradabad.
J. L. S. Peshaur (likely this, and not *P. canariensis*).
Stocks. Beluchistan, above 4000 feet.
Griff. Afghan.

PANICEÆ.

1303. PASPALUM PEDICELLATUM, *Nees.*
Milium sanguinale, *Roxb.*
T. T. Moradabad.

1304. P. ROYLEANUM, *Nees.*
T. T. Moradabad ; Punjab.

1305. P. SCROBICULATUM, *L.*
P. Kora, *Willd.*
Edgew. Seikh Protected States, cult. ; Multan, cult., " Kodon."
T. T. Moradabad ; Punjab.
Jacq. Punjab.
J. L. S. Peshaur.

1306. MILIUM EFFUSUM, *L.*
M. nepalense, *Royle.*
T. T. Garwhal ; Simla.

1307. ERIOCHLOA ANNULATA, *Kth.*
T. T. Moradabad, *Ganges.*

1308. UROCHLOA.
Coridochloa fimbriata, *Nees.*
T. T. Moradabad.
Jacq. Punjab, No. 129 ; Rajaori, No. 135.

1309. PANICUM ANTIDOTALE, *Retz.*
Edgew. Multan.

T. T. Seharanpur ; Punjab.
Jacq. Seharanpur.
A. Jhelum.
Stocks. Sindh.
Frere. Beluchistan.

1310. P. BRIZOIDES, *Jacq.*
Edgew. Multan ; Seikh States.
T. T. Kumaon ; Moradabad.
Jacq. Calcutta.

1311. P. DISTACHYON, *L.*
T. T. Moradabad ; Punjab.
Jacq. Punjab, No. 145.

1312. P. FLUITANS, *L.*
T. T. Lahore.
Stocks. Sindh.

1313. P. HELOPUS, *Trin.*
T. T. Punjab ; Moradabad.

1314. P. HIRSUTUM, *Koen.*
P. helopus, *Trin.*
Edgew. Seikh Protected States.
T. T. Lahore ; Moradabad.

1315. P. HUMILE, *Nees.*
T. T. Punjab.

1316. P. HYDASPICUM, *Edgew.*
Edgew. Multan.

1317. P. MAXIMUM, *Jacq.*
T. T. Moradabad.
J. L. S. Peshaur.
Stocks. Sindh.

1318. P. MILIACEUM, *L.*
Royle. North-west provinces, cultivated, "Cheena."
Edgew. Multan, cult.
T. T. Cultivated, Moradabad ; Punjab ; western Thibet and Iskardo.
J. L. S. Peshaur, cult.
Stocks. Beluchistan and Sindh, cult.
Griff. Afghan.
Edgew. Seikh States, "Chini," cult. (may be this).

1319. P. MILIARE, *Lamarck.*
Edgew. North-west India ; Multan, cult.
T. T. Punjab ; Moradabad.

1320. P. NEPALENSE, *Spr.*
P. plicatum, *Roxb.*
Royle. North-west India.
T. T. Moradabad.

1321. P. PETIVERII, *Trin.*
T. T. Punjab ; Moradabad.
Jacq. Rajaori.
A. Jhelum.
Stocks. Sindh.
Griff. Afghan.

1322. P. PROSTRATUM, *Lamarck.*
P. procumbens, *Nees.*
P. setigerum, *Roxb.*
Edgew. Multan (*Oplismenus prostratus*).
T. T. Punjab ; Moradabad.
A. Jhelum.

1323. P. PSILOPODIUM, *Trin.*
Edgew. Multan.
T. T. Punjab ; Chenab, near Sealkote.

1324. P. REPENS, *L.*
P. paludosum, *Roxb.*
T. T. Moradabad ; Punjab ; Lahore.
J. L. S. Peshaur.

1325. PANICUM, sp.
No. 29, *Hook. fil. & T. T. hb. Ind. or.*
T. T. Moradabad ; Punjab ; south of Lahore.

1326. P. TENERIFFÆ, *R. Br.*
Stocks. Sindh.

1327. P. VESTITUM, *Nees.*
P. coccospermum, *Steud.*
Edgew. Multan.
T. T. Punjab ; Garwhal ; Simla Hills.

1328. PANICUM.
Digitaria ciliaris, *Nees.*
Edgew. Multan.
T. T. Moradabad ; Punjab ; Lahore.
Stocks. Sindh.

Var. *β.* VILLOSA.
Jacq. Punjab.
Stocks. Sindh.
Griff. Afghan.

1329. PANICUM SANGUINALE, *L.*
Digitaria sanguinalis, *Scop.*
Edgew. Multan (*sanguinolenta*, perhaps this).
T. T. Punjab; Lahore.
A. Jhelum.

Var. β. ÆGYPTIACA, *Lam.*
P. ægyptiaca.
T. T. Punjab.

Var. γ. EXTENSUM, *Nees.*
T. T. Moradabad; Punjab.

1330. ISACHNE AUSTRALIS, *Br.*
Jacq. Rajaori.

1331. OPLISMENUS COLONUS, *Kth.*
Echinochloa colona, *Kth.*
Panicum colonum, *L.*
T. T. Moradabad.
Edgew. Multan; Seikh Protected States.
A. Jhelum, also cult.
J. L. S. Peshaur.
Edgew. Seikh States, "Junglee-Sawank."
A. Jhelum, "Shamack."

1332. O. COMPOSITUS, *R. & S.*
T. T. Deobund; Simla.
Jacq. Punjab; Rajaori.

1333. O. FRUMENTACEUS, *Link.*
Panicum frumentaceum, *Roxb.*
Edgew. Seikh Protected States, cult., "Sawank."
T. T. Moradabad, cult.; Punjab.
Stocks. Beluchistan to Kurrachee.
Griff. Beluchistan; Afghan.

1334. O. LATIFOLIUS, *R. & S.*
T. T. Simla.
Jacq. Punjab.

1335. O. STAGNINUS, *Kunth.*
Panicum stagninum, *L.*
P. crus-galli, *L.*
P. hispidulum, *Roxb.*
Edgew. Multan.
T. T. Moradabad; Punjab.
J. L. S. Peshaur.
Frere. Beluchistan.
Griff. Afghan.

1336. **Pennisetum araneosum**, *Edgew.*
J. L. S. Peshaur.

1337. **P. cenchroides**, *Rich.*
P. rufescens, *Spr.*
Cenchrus echinoides, *Wt.* (*Hb. Royle*).
Royle. Northern India; Delhi.
Edgew. Multan (*P. cenchri*).
T. T. Punjab; Moradabad; Ferozepur.
A. Jhelum.
J. L. S. Peshaur.
Stocks. Sindh.
Frere. Beluchistan.

1338. **P. dichotomum**, *Del.*
J. L. S. Peshaur.
Stocks. Sindh.

1339. **P. sinaicum**, *Decais.*
A. Jhelum.
Griff. Afghan.

1340. **P. triflorum**, *Nees.*
T. T. Punjab; Simla; Rampur.

1341. **Setaria glauca**, *Beauv.*
Edgew. Multan.
T. T. Punjab; Moradabad; Lahore.
A. Jhelum.
J. L. S. Peshaur.

1342. **S. intermedia**, *R. & S.*
T. T. Moradabad; Punjab.

1333. **S. italica**, *Kth.*
Edgew. Multan, cult.
T. T. Punjab, cult.; western Thibet, cult.
J. L. S. Peshaur, cult.
Stocks. Sindh (cult.?). Italian Millet.

1344. **S. verticillata**, *Beauv.*
Edgew. Multan.
T. T. Moradabad; Punjab; Lahore.
Stocks. Sindh; Beluchistan.
Frere. Beluchistan.

1345. **S. viridis**, *Beauv.*
Fleming. Marri.
Griff. Afghan.

1346. GYMNOTHRIX FLACCIDA, *Munro.*
T. T. Jamu Hills.

1347. PENICILLARIA SPICATA, *Lindl.*
P. cylindrica, *R. & S.*
Edgew. Multan; Seikh Protected States, cultivated, "Bajra."
T. T. Lahore and Moradabad, cult.
Jacq. Punjab, cult.
A. Jhelum, Hushiarpur, and Punjab generally, cultivated very largely. "Bajree."
J. L. S. Peshaur.
Stocks. Sindh, cult.

1348. CENCHRUS TRIFLORUS, *Roxb.*
C. Schimperi, *Hochst. & St.*
Royle. Delhi.
T. T. Punjab, Lahore.
Stocks. Beluchistan.
Frere. Beluchistan.

1349. C. ECHINATUS, *L.*
Edgew. Multan.
J. L. S. Peshaur.
Edgew. Seikh Protected States. "*Cenchrus* sp., as well as a species of *Pennisetum*, both called, 'Dhaman,' are good fodder-grasses."

1350. C. MONTANUS, *Nees.*
Royle. North-west India.
Edgew. Multan.
T. T. Punjab Sirhind, Loodiana.

1351. LAPPAGO RACEMOSA, *Willd.*
L. biflora, *Roxb.*
Edgew. Multan.
T. T. Punjab, Moradabad.
A. Jhelum.
J. L. S. Peshaur.
Stocks. Sindh.
Frere. Beluchistan.

1352. LATIPES SENEGALENSIS, *Kth.*
Stocks. Sindh.
Frere. Beluchistan.

Stipeæ.

1353. **Aristida articulata**, ***Edgew.***
Edgew. **Multan.**

1354. **A. depressa**, ***Retz.***
A. setacea, ***Retz.***
T. T. **Punjab; Moradabad; Lahore.**
Jacq. **Punjab, No. 195, 198.**
J. L. S. **Peshaur.**
A. **Jhelum.**

1355. **A. funiculata**, ***Trin.***
(Referred by Munro to ***Aristida murina,*** **Cav.)**
Edgew. **Multan.**

1356. **A. hirti-gluma**, ***Steud.***
A. ciliata, ***Hochst.***
Edgew. **Multan.**
Griff. **Afghan.**

1357. **A. hystricula**, ***Edgew.***
Edgew. **Multan.**

1358. **A. mallica**, ***Edgew.***
Edgew. **Multan.**

1359. **A. murina**, ***Cav.***
A. Royleana, ***Trin.***
A. Hystrix, ***L. fil.***
A. funiculata, ***Trin.*** **(*Munro*).**
Edgew. **Multan (*Arthratherum Royleanum*); and Multan (*Aristida funiculata,* Trin.).**
T. T. **Punjab, Lahore.**
Jacq. **Punjab.**
A. **Jhelum.**

1360. **A. plumosa**, ***L.***
A. pogonoptilum, ***Jb. et Sp.***
Edgew. **Multan.**
Jacq. **Punjab.**
Stocks. **Beluch., no. 638.**
Griff. **Afghan.**

1361. **Aristida**, **species.**
Herb. Hook. fil. et T. T. Ind. or. **no. 4.**
Stocks. **Sindh.**
Frere. **Beluchistan.**

1362. A. VULGARIS, *Trin.*
A. cærulescens, *Desf.*
Chætaria vulgaris, *var.* cærulescens, *Edgew.*
Edgew. Multan.
Stocks. Beluchistan.
Griff. Afghan.

AGROSTEÆ.

1363. SPOROBOLUS COMMUTATUS, *Knth.*
Edgew. Multan.
T. T. Lahore; Punjab.
Griff. Afghan.

1364. S. DIANDER, *Beauv.*
T. T. Moradabad; Punjab; Chenab; Simla.
Jacq. Rajaori.

1365. S. GENICULATUS, *Nees.*
T. T. Punjab; Moradabad.

1366. S. PALLIDUS, *Nees.*
S. (Vilfa) pallidus, *Lind.*
Edgew. Multan.
T. T. Punjab; Moradabad.
Stocks. Sindh.

1367. SPOROBOLUS, species.
No. 7, *Herb. Hook. f. et T. T. Ind. or.*
Stocks. Sindh.

1368. AGROSTIS ALBA, *L.*
T. T. Iskardo.
Jacq. Kumaon; Kashmir.
Griff. Afghan.
J. L. S. Peshaur.

1369. VILFA SCABRIFOLIA, *Hochst.*
Herb. Edgew. No. 2302 ('Flora Multan').
Stocks. No. 677.
Edgew. Multan.
Stocks. Sindh.

1370. POLYPOGON MONSPELIENSIS, *Desf.*
Edgew. Multan.
T. T. Punjab; Moradabad; Lahore.
Jacq. Malwa.

A. Jhelum.
J. L. S. Peshaur.
Stocks. Beluchistan.
Griff. Afghan.

Arundineæ.

1371. Arundo donax, *L.*
A. bengalensis, *Retz.*
Edgew. Multan.
T. T. Punjab.
A. Jhelum, and cult. in gardens; Hushiarpur, "Sukna."
Stocks. Beluchistan.
Griff. Afghan.

1372. A. phragmites, *L.*
T. T. Lahore; south of Ferozepur.

1373. Arundo Karka, *Roxb.*
A. (Phragmites) Roxburghii, *Steud.*
Edgew. Multan.
T. T. Punjab; Moradabad; Lahore; Rampur.
Jacq. Rajaori.
J. L. S. Peshaur.
Stocks. Sindh.

Pappophoreæ.

1374. Pappophorum arabicum, *Hochst.*
Edgew. Multan.

1375. P. nanum, *Steud.*
P. vincentianum, *Schmidt.*
Edgew. Multan; Chandnot Hills.

1376. P. persicum, *Boiss.*
Edgew. Multan.

Chlorideæ.

1377. Schœnefeldia pallida, *Edgew.*
S. gracilis, *Kunth.*
Edgew. Multan.

1378. Cynodon dactylon, *Pers.*
Edgew. Multan (*linearis*, Willd.); Seikh Protected States, very rare in in sandy parts. "Dhub."
T. T. Moradabad; Lahore.

A. Jhelum; Hushiarpur; throughout the Punjab the most common grass; in some localities not so, as west of Pind-Dadun-Khan. "Doob."
J. L. S. Peshaur.
Stocks. Sindh; Beluchistan.
Frere. Beluchistan.
Griff. Afghan.

1379. DACTYLOCTENIUM ÆGYPTIACUM, *Willd.*
Edgew. Multan.
T. T. Punjab; Moradabad; Lahore.
A. Jhelum.
Stocks. Sindh.
Frere. Beluchistan.

Var. MUCRONATUM.
Edgew. Multan.

1380. CHLORIS BARBATA, *Swartz.*
T. T. Moradabad.
Vicary. Sindh.

1381. C. MECCANA, *Hochst. & St.*
T. T. Moradabad.
Frere. Beluchistan.

1382. C. VILLOSA, *Pers.*
Edgew. Multan; Shakote.
Vicary. Boogta Hills.
J. L. S. Peshaur.
Stocks. Sindh.
Griff. Afghan.

1383. LEPTOCHLOA ARABICA, *Knth.*
Edgew. Multan (named *Dinebra verticillata* in 'Multan Flora').
Griff. Afghan; Jellalabad.

1384. L. FILIFORMIS, *R. & S.*
L. tenerrima, *R & S.*
T. T. Punjab; Lahore; Moradabad.

1385. ELEUSINE ARABICA, *Hochst. & St.*
E. flagellifera, *Nees.*
Edgew. Multan.
T. T. Punjab.
Jacq. No. 245, Punjab.
J. L. S. Peshaur.
Stocks. Sindh.
Griff. Afghan.

1386. E. CORACANA, *Gaert.*
Edgew. Multan and Seikh Protected States, cult. "Mandua," and is the "Kodon" of the hill people.
T. T. Punjab; Moradabad.
Stocks. Sindh.

1387. E. INDICA, *L.*
T. T. Moradabad.

1388. E. VERTICILLATA, *Roxb.*
Dinebra verticillata, *Wight.*
Leptochloa verticillata, *Knth.*
T. T. Punjab; Sutlej valley; Rampur; Lahore.

1389. MELANOCENCHRIS ROYLEANA, *Nees.*
Eutriana abyssinica, *Br.*
Royle. North-west India.
A. Jhelum.
Stocks. Sindh.

AVENEÆ.

1390. AVENA FATUA, *L.*
Edgew. Multan.
T. T. Punjab.
A. Jhelum; Salt range. "Gundal."
J. L. S. Peshaur.
Stocks. Indus basin.
Griff. Afghan.

1391. A. SATIVA, *L.*
Hook. fil. Sikkim, cult. 7000 to 12,000 feet.
A. Oats occasionally cult. by Europeans in the Punjab.

1392. TRISTACHYA BARBATA, *Steud.*
T. Stocksii, *Munro.*
Stocks. Sindh.

FESTUCEÆ.

1393. POA ANNUA, *L.*
Edgew. Multan.
T. T. Punjab.
J. L. S. Peshaur.

1394. **ÆLUROPUS VILLOSUS**, ***Trin.***
A. repens, *Parl.*
Dactylis repens, *Desf.*
Edgew. **Multan (*nilotica*, perhaps for *niliaca?*).**
A. **Jhelum.**
Stocks. **Sindh.**

1395. **ÆLUROPUS.**
Brizopyrum mucronatum, *Nees.*
Stocks. **Sindh.**

1396. **ERAGROSTIS BROWNEI, *Nees.***
Edgew. **Multan.**
T. T. **Moradabad; Seharanpur; Lahore.**

1397. **E. CILIARIS, *L.***
Poa ciliata, *Roxb.*
T. T. **Punjab; Moradabad.**
Stocks. **Sindh.**

1398. **E. CYLINDRICA, *Nees.***
T. T. **Moradabad.**

1399. **E. CYNOSUROIDES, *Retz.***
Edgew. **Multan.**
T. T. **Punjab; Moradabad.**
A. **Jhelum.**
J. L. S. **Peshaur.**
Stocks. **Sindh.**

1400. **E. DIANDRA, *Roxb.***
Edgew. **Multan.**
T. T. **Moradabad.**

1401. **E. MEGASTACHYA, *Link.***
T. T. **Moradabad; Meerut; Jamu.**
Stocks. **Sindh.**
Frere. **Beluchistan.**

1402. **E. MULTIFLORA, *Nees.***
E. tremula, *Munro.*
Edgew. **Multan.**
T. T. **Punjab.**
Griff. **Afghan.**

1403. **E. NUTANS, *Roxb.***
E. interrupta, *Roxb.*
Edgew. **Multan.**
T. T. **Punjab; Lahore.**
Stocks. **Beluch.**

1404. E. PILOSA, *Beauv.*
Royle. Seharanpur.
T. T. Seharanpur; Punjab.

1405. E. PLUMOSA, *Link.*
Poa tenella, *L.*
P. viscosa, *Willd. & Retz.*
Edgew. Multan.
T. T. Moradabad; Punjab; Jamu; Lahore.
A. Jhelum.
Griff. Afghan.

1406. E. POÆOIDES, *Beauv.*
Poa eragrostis, *L.*
Edgew. Multan.
T. T. Moradabad; Seharanpur; Punjab; Lahore.
A. Jhelum.
J. L. S. Peshaur.
Stocks. Beluchistan.
Griff. Afghan.

1407. E. UNIOLOIDES, *Nees.*
Edgew. Multan.
T. T. Moradabad; Simla.
Jacq. Deccan.

1408. E. VERTICILLATA, *Beauv.*
(Very near *E. pilosa,* Beauv.)
T. T. Punjab; Moradabad.
A. Jhelum.
Frere. Beluchistan.
Griff. Afghan.

1409. KŒLERIA CRISTATA, *Pers.*
T. T. Kumaon.
St. & W. Kumaon.
Jacq. Kashmir.
J. L. S. Peshaur.

1410. K. PHLEOIDES, *Pers.*
Edgew. Ferozepur.
T. T. Lahore; Ferozepur.
A. Jhelum.
J. L. S. Peshaur.

1411. LAMARCKIA AUREA, *Mœnch.*
Vicary. Peshaur.
J. L. S. Peshaur.
Griff. Afghan.

1412. ELYTROPHORUS ARTICULATUS, *Beauv.*
T. T. Moradabad.

1413. BROMUS MOLLIS, *L.*
J. L. S. Peshaur?

1414. B. ARVENSIS, *L.*
T. T. Simla.
Lady Dalhousie. Simla.
A. Jhelum.
Stocks. Beluchistan.
Griff. Afghan.

1415. BAMBUSA, sp.
Edgew. Multan, cult.
A. A lofty bamboo is cultivated near dwellings in the ranges of hills, Hushiarpur district, as also at Hushiarpur.

1416. DENDROCALAMUS STRICTUS, *Nees.*
Bambusa stricta, *Roxb. Corom. Plants* as to the description, but not plate (see *Munro, in Linn. Trans.* vol. xxvi. p. 147).
Strachey. Kumaon.
T. T. Kalka.
A. Jhelum, valleys of Mount Tilla (not *B. arundinacea,* as in 'Jhelum Flora'); Hushiarpur district, forms a dense jungle.
Falconer. Dehra-Doon.
A. "Bans," "Bansa." This is also cultivated about Hushiarpur.

HORDEACEÆ.

1417. LOLIUM TEMULENTUM, *L.*
Edgew. Multan.
T. T. Lahore; Moradabad.
Jacq. Punjab.
J. L. S. Peshaur.
Stocks. Sindh.
Griff. Afghan.

1418. TRITICUM VULGARE, *Vill.*
A. Wheat is largely cultivated throughout the Punjab, occasionally to 9000 feet; Lahul. "Gehun," "Kunuck."
Edgew. Varieties cult. at Multan, *æstivum, hybernum,* "Durun."

1419. HORDEUM VULGARE, *L.*, var. ÆGICERAS.
T. T. Great heights in western Thibet.

Var. HEXASTICHON.
A. Largely cultivated throughout the Punjab. Barley, "Jhou."

ROTTBŒLLIACEÆ.

1420. **NARDUS STRICTA**, *L.*
J. L. S. Peshaur.

1421. **HEMARTHRIA COMPRESSA**, *Br.*
Rottbœllia glabra, *Roxb.*
T. T. Punjab; Moradabad.
Griff. Afghan.

1422. **MNESITHEA LÆVIS**, *Kth.*
Rottbœllia perforata, *Roxb.*
T. T. Moradabad; Punjab.

1423. **ROTTBŒLLIA EXALTATA**, *L.*
T. T. Moradabad; Kumaon, 4500 feet.

ANDROPOGONEÆ.

1454. **PEROTIS LATIFOLIA**, *Ait.*
Edgew. Seikh Protected States.
T. T. Moradabad; Punjab; Lahore.
Griff. Afghan.

1425. **ERIOCHRYSIS NARENGA**, *Nees.*
Saccharum Narenga, *Ham.*
T. T. Punjab; Rowlee Ghat.

1426. **SACCHARUM SARA**, *Roxb.*
S. Munja, *Roxb.*
Edgew. Multan.
T. T. Moradabad; Lahore.
Jacq. Punjab.
A. Jhelum; Hushiarpur; Indus river. At Jhelum, the land on which this ("Moonj") grows is protected, as the fibre brings a fair price in the market.

1427. **S. SPONTANEUM**, *L.*
S. canaliculatum, *Roxb.*
S. ægyptiacum, *Willd.*
Royle. Northern India.
Edgew. Multan.
T. T. Moradabad; Punjab; Lahore.
A. Jhelum; Sindh; Hushiarpur.
Stocks. Sindh.
Griff. Afghan.
A. Jhelum, "Kha," "Khans;" Sindhee, "Khans."

1428. S. OFFICINARUM, *L.*

A. Sugar-cane, "Gunnah." Cultivated throughout the Punjab, chiefly in its south-eastern parts, as the Seikh Protected States (*Edgew.*), Hushiarpur (*A.*), and on the margins of the rivers. Largely eaten by the natives in the stick, and thus a very common bazar commodity.

1429. IMPERATA ARUNDINACEA, *Cyrill.*
I. cylindrica, *Beauv.*
I. Kœnigii, *Beauv.*
Saccharum cylindricum, *Lam.*
Edgew. Multan; Seikh Protected States.
T. T. Punjab; Lahore; Moradabad.
A. Jhelum; Hushiarpur; Indus river; Sindh.
J. L. S. Peshaur.
Stocks. Sindh; Beluchistan.
Griff. Afghan.

1430. POGONATHERUM CRINITUM, *Trin.*
T. T. Jamu; Upper Punjab.
Jacq. Agra.

1431. ERIANTHUS, species.
No. 14, *Hook. list.*
T. T. Afghan.
Stocks. Beluchistan.
Griff. Affghan.

1432. ERIANTHUS AUREUS, *Nees.*
T. T. Moradabad.

1433. E. RAVENNÆ, *Beauv.*
Saccharum Ravennæ, *L.*
Edgew. Multan.
T. T. Rowlee Ghat; Kumaon; Punjab.
Griff. Afghan.

1434. ELIONURUS HIRSUTUS, *Vahl.*
Rotthœllia hirsuta, *Vahl.*
Edgew. Multan.
Jacq. Punjab; Jelallpur.
J. L. S. Peshaur.
Stocks. Sindh; Beluchistan.
Griff. Afghan.

1435. ANTHISTIRIA ANATHERA, *Nees.*
T. T. Simla.
Lady Dalhousie. Simla.
A. Jhelum.
Jacq. Kashmir; Rajaori.

1436. A. WIGHTII, *Nees.*
T. T. Moradabad; Punjab.

1437. APLUDA COMMUNIS, *Nees.*
A. aristata, *Roxb.* (*Edgew.*)
Edgew. Multan.
T. T. Kalka; Jamu.
Jacq. Rajmahal.
J. L. S. Peshaur.

1438. A. ARISTATA, *L.*
A. rostrata, *Nees.*
T. T. Rampur.
Jacq. Rajaori.

1439. A. GENICULATA, *Roxb.*
T. T. Jamu.
J. L. S. Peshaur.

1440. BATRATHERUM ECHINATUM, *Heyne.*
Jacq. Punjab; Himalaya.

1441. B. MOLLE, *Nees.*
T. T. Kumaon.
St. & Wint. Kumaon, 4000 ft.
A. Jhelum; Hushiarpur.

1442. ANATHERUM MURICATUM, *Beauv.*
Vetiveria odorata, *Virey.*
Andropogon muricatum, *Retz.*
Edgew. Multan; Seikh Protected States. "Senth."
T. T. Punjab; Lahore; Moradabad.
A. Jhelum, on land near Russool, protected, "Khus-Kus."
J. L. S. Peshaur.

1443. CYMBOPOGON ARRIANI, *Edgew.*
Edgew. Multan.

1444. C FLEXUOSUS, *Nees.*
T. T. Moradabad; Seharanpur; Rampur; Rechnab Doab.

1445. C. LANIGER, *Desf.*
C. Iwarancusa, *Blane.*
Andropogon Iwarancusa, *Roxb.*
T. T. Punjab; Lahore.

Jacq. Agra.
A. Jhelum.
J. L. S. Peshaur.
Stocks. Sindh.

1446. C. MARTINI, *Munro.*
Andropogon Martini, *Roxb.*
A. nardoides, *Nees.*
Calamus aromaticus, *Royle.*
Andropogon Schœnanthus, *L.* (not of *Wall.*) *fid. Munro.*
Royle, Delhi, North-west Provinces, India. "Yields the grass oil of Nimar."
A. Is cultivated in Punjab gardens (no specimens).

1447. SORGHUM HALEPENSE, *L.*
Edgew. Multan.
T. T. Simla; Punjab.
J. L. S. Peshaur.
Griff. Afghan.

1448. S. MUTICUM, *Nees, in hb. Wight.*
T. T. Moradabad; Simla; Punjab.

1449. S. VULGARE, *Pers.*
Holcus Sorghum, *L.*
Edgew. Multan, cult.; Seikh Protected States, "Joar."
T. T. Moradabad, cult., "Jowara."
A. Cultivated over all the Punjab, "Jowar."
J. L. S. Peshaur, cult.
Griff. Afghan.

1450. ANDROPOGON ANNULATUS, *Forsk.*
Edgew. Multan.
T. T. Punjab; Moradabad.
A. Jhelum.
Frere. Beluchistan.

Var. PUNCTATUS, *Roxb.*
T. T. Moradabad; Rechnab Doab; Punjab.

1451. A. BLADHII, *Retz.*
Edgew. Multan; Seikh Protected States.
T. T. Moradabad; Lahore.
Jacq. Delhi to Bombay; Neemuch.
J. L. S. Peshaur.
Griff. Afghan.

1452. A. FOVEOLATUS, *DC.*
T. T. Punjab.
Stocks. Sindh.

1453. A. ISCHÆNUM, *L.*
T. T. Simla.
Stocks. Beluchistan.
Griff. Afghan.

1454. A. PERTUSUS, *Willd.*
A. scandens, *Roxb.*
Edgew. Multan; Seikh Protected Stat
T. T. Moradabad; Punjab; Lahore.

1455. CHRYSOPOGON GRYLLUS, *Trin.*
Andropogon Gryllus, *L.*
A. Royleanus, *Nees.*
T. T. Simla.
J. L. S. Peshaur.

1456. C. SERRULATUS, *Trin.*
T. T. Moradabad; Simla; Jamu.
Jacq. Rajaori.
A. Jhelum.

1457. HETEROPOGON CONTORTUS, *R. & S.*
Andropogon contortus, *L.*
Edgew. Seikh Protected States.
T. T. Moradabad; Kumaon; Punjab.
Jacq. Rajaori; Agra.
A. Jhelum.
J. L. S. Peshaur.

1458. SPODIOPOGON ANGUSTIFOLIUS, *Trin.*
Andropogon involutus, *Steud.*
T. T. Kumaon.
Jacq. Punjab.

ACOTYLEDONÆ.

ACROGENÆ.

FILICES.

1459. CERATOPTERIS THALICTROIDES, *Bung.*
Jacq. Punjab.

1460. ADIANTUM CAUDATUM, *L.*
T. T. Jamu; Chenab.
Edgew. Multan; Adali valley; Punjab.
Fleming. Salt range.
A. Jhelum; Mt. Tilla; Hushiarpur.

1461. A. CAPILLUS VENERIS, *L.*
Edgew. Multan, in wells.
T. T. Punjab.
Fleming. Salt range.
A. Jhelum; Hushiarpur; Loodiana; Philor; Umritsur, common in old wells.
J. L. S. Peshaur, sides of ditches.
Stocks. Sindh; Beluchistan.
Griff. Afghan.

1462. CHEILANTHES DALHOUSIÆ, *Hook.*
Edgew. Simla.
St. & Wint. Kumaon.
A. Jhelum; Mt. Tilla; Hushiarpur.

1463. C. FARINOSA, *Kaulf.*
T. T. Jamu.
Edgew. Simla.
A. Jhelum; Hushiarpur.
Stocks. Sindh.

1464. C. SZOVITZII, *F. & M.*
Vicary. Peshaur.
Stocks. Beluchistan.
Griff. Afghan.

1465. C. FRAGRANS, *L.*
T. T. Jamu.
Fleming. Marri.
Griff. Afghan.

1466. **Pteris longifolia**, *L.*
T. T. Nynee-tal; Chamba.
Fleming. Punjab; Salt range.
J. L. S. Peshaur.
Stocks. Bombay.

1467. **Actinopteris radiata**, *Link.*
Asplenium radiatum, *Swartz.*
Royle. Delhi.
T. T. Moradabad.
Jacq. Delhi; Ajmere.
Stocks. Sindh.

1468. **Nephrodium Thelypteris**, *Desv.*
Jacq. Kashmir.
J. L. S. Peshaur.

1469. **Lastræa**, species.
A. Hushiarpur; Purwain range, rare.

1470. **Polypodium proliferum**, *Presl.*
T. T. Moradabad.
St. & Wint. Kumaon plains.

EQUISETACEÆ.

1471. **Equisetum debile**, *Roxb.*
T. T. Punjab.
A. (*G. Henderson*). Jhelum; Hushiarpur.
J. L. S. Peshaur.
Stocks. Indus basin.

CHARACEÆ.

1472. **Chara**, species.
T. T. Punjab.
A. (*Henderson*). Jhelum.
J. L. S. Peshaur.
Stocks. Indus basin.

MARSILEACEÆ.

1473. MARSILEA EROSA, *Willd.* (not QUADRIFOLIA, *L.*)
Edgew. Multan.
T. T. Punjab.
A. Jhelum; Hushiarpur.
J. L. S. Peshaur.
Stocks. Sindh; Indus basin.

1474. AZOLLA, sp.
J. L. S. Peshaur.

1475. SALVINIA, sp.
J. L. S. Peshaur.

MUSCI.

1476. PHASCUM, sp.
Edgew. Multan.
J. L. S. Peshaur.
Griff. Punjab, on sand banks.
Stocks. Indus basin.

MARCHANTIACEÆ.

1477. MARCHANTIA, sp.
J. L. S. Peshaur.

RICCIACEÆ.

1478. RICCIA FLUITANS.
J. L. S. Peshaur.

1479. R. NATANS.
J. L. S. Peshaur.

THALLOGENÆ.

FUNGI.

1480. AGARICUS, sp.

A. On Grand-Trunk road, between Jhelum and Goojerat, at a horse-chokee, found a mushroom, edible and very like *A. campestris.*

Some seasons in February, at Jacobabad, Sindh, immense quantities of an edible mushroom spring up; this is eaten by Europeans. The natives collect a kind of morelle and eat it (*H. R. M'Dougall*).

1481. MORCHELLA, species.

Edgew. Multan, resembling a morelle, called "Kumbha," is eaten and liked by Europeans, and is from the desert.

Another called "Boenphul," or earth-fruit, found in cultivated land, is also eaten.

T. T. Imported largely into the bazars of Northern India from Kashm is a morell called "Kana-Kuchua."

ALGÆ.

1482. CONFERVA, sp.

J. L. S. Peshaur.

INDEX.

The classes, natural orders, and genera are paged; species and synonyms numbered according to the number in the Catalogue.

Synonyms are in *italics*. Some names are in *italics* that are not synonyms, and are similarly referred to Catalogue number, where it will be seen why they have been introduced,—as, for instance, Bambusa *arundinacea*, 1416 *arundinacea* is not a synonym for the species 1416, but was the name applied in my Jhelum list to number 1416 of this list; and at 1416 the error is corrected.

English and native synonyms are not in *italics*, and are referred to Catalogue number.

THE END.